1 MONTH OF FREE READING

at

www.ForgottenBooks.com

By purchasing this book you are eligible for one month membership to ForgottenBooks.com, giving you unlimited access to our entire collection of over 700,000 titles via our web site and mobile apps.

To claim your free month visit: www.forgottenbooks.com/free147663

Similar Books Are Available from
www.forgottenbooks.com

MASSACHUSETTS

IN THE

WOMAN SUFFRAGE MOVEMENT

In the administration of a State, neither a woman as a woman, nor a man as a man, has any special function, but the gifts are equally diffused in both sexes. * * * One woman has the gift of healing, another not; one is a musician, another not a musician; one woman is a philosopher, and another is an enemy to philosophy. * * The same education and opportunity for self-development which makes man a good guardian (or ruler) will make woman a good guardian (or ruler); for their original nature is the same.

PLATO, *Rep. B. V.*

MASSACHUSETTS

IN THE

OMAN SUFFRAGE MOVEMENT.

GENERAL, POLITICAL, LEGAL AND LEGISLATIVE
HISTORY FROM 1774, TO 1881.

BY

HARRIET H. ROBINSON.

The woman's hour has struck.—"WARRINGTON."

BOSTON:
ROBERTS BROTHERS.
1881.

TO

THE YOUNG WOMEN OF MASSACHUSETTS

WHO ENJOY THE FRUITS OF THE LABORS OF THOSE
WHOSE NAMES ARE RECORDED IN THESE PAGES

I Dedicate this Book

WITH THE HOPE THAT SINCE THEY FIND THE PATH SO
WELL OPENED TO THEM FOR BETTER EDUCATIONAL,
SOCIAL, AND POLITICAL ADVANTAGES, THEY
MAY BEAR IN MIND HOW MUCH

THE WOMAN'S RIGHTS MOVEMENT

HAS DONE TO CLEAR THE WAY.

CONTENTS.

INTRODUCTION.

THE writing of this book has been a labor of love; and I publish it in the hope that it may be found useful as a book of reference, and also, that it may help to keep the memory green of some of the earlier workers in the Woman's Rights Movement.

When writing upon certain phases of this question, I have often been very much hampered for want of authentic data upon which to base my statements. The cyclopædias say comparatively little, and there is no book of reference that enters into details on this subject. The need of such a book has no doubt been felt by others as well as by myself, and I sincerely hope that, so far as it goes, this work will supply that need.

In 1870, when I began to work for woman suffrage, I found in the ranks, many earnest men and women who had labored long in the weedy field of this reform. There were also, dim traditions of others whose names were half forgotten and the memory of whose services was fast becoming obliterated. A reformer is the Rip Van Winkle in the history of his time. If he leaves the procession, remains inactive for a period of years, or dies. he and his work are very soon forgotten. Already, the names of many of those who helped to lead the anti-slavery movement are to be found only in dusty reports or files of old newspapers. Without an authentic record of the woman suffrage movement, the coming generation might in a similar way forget its early workers.

In presenting the part Massachusetts has taken, I have described its aspect as one who sees a landscape from a height—the general effect has been given, instead of minute details upon single points. I have not dwelt upon individual action, nor made a record of the work done by the leaders, since this is the province of the biographer rather than that of the historian. I should gladly have devoted some space to the doctrine of woman's rights, as expounded by those whose names are found in these pages; but within the limits of this book it would have been impossible to do justice to such authors or to such a theme.

My sources of information have been, carefully preserved reports of meetings; legislative documents and records; "Warrington's" letters and writings in the *Springfield Republican, New York Tribune,* and other newspapers; letters from friends of the cause from all parts of the country, and the personal reminiscences of old-time workers.   To all the friends who have aided me in collecting material, I desire to express my thanks.   I am especially grateful to Louisa M. Alcott and Wendell Phillips for their encouragement, and sympathy with my work ; also to Frank B. Sanborn and Samuel E. Sewall, who have kindly helped me in the revision of my proofs, and thus secured for these pages, technical and legal accuracy.

H. H. R.

Toiling,— rejoicing,— sorrowing,
  Onward. through life he goes;
Each morning. sees some task begun,
  Each evening. sees it close;
Something attempted, something done,
  Has earned. a night's repose.

—LONGFELLOW.

MASSACHUSETTS

IN THE

WOMAN SUFFRAGE MOVEMENT.

———•———

CHAPTER I.

GENERAL HISTORY — EARLY INFLUENCES.
1774—1850.

We want powder, but by the blessing of Heaven we fear them not. ABIGAIL ADAMS, in 1774.

IN this brief history of the Woman Suffrage Movement in Massachusetts, will be found a record of the distant and surrounding causes which brought the reform into successful existence, with some mention of the names of those men and women who, long before the date of the first Woman's Rights Convention, listened and responded to this new cry for life.

The earliest voice heard was that of Abigail

Adams, wife of our first President Adams, who, in a letter written to her husband, in 1774, at the time the First Continental Congress met in Phila-adelphia, said: "In the new code of laws * * I desire you would remember the ladies, and be more generous and favorable to them than your ancestors. Do not put such unlimited power in the hands of the husbands. Remember, all men would be tyrants if they could. If particular care and attention is not paid to the ladies, we are determined to foment a rebellion, and will not hold ourselves· bound by any laws in which we have no voice or representation." Was not this a prophetic word? and though spoken half playfully by one who, perhaps, would not have confessed how serious the matter was with her, to-day, after an interval of more than a century, it contains the gist of the whole Woman's Rights Movement.

After the Constitution was framed, the women who had done and sacrificed so much for the country, in the War of Independence, having been left out, Mrs. Adams wrote again to her hus-band in gentle warning words: "I cannot say that I think you are very generous to the ladies, for, while you are proclaiming peace and good will to all men, emancipating all nations, you insist upon retaining absolute power over wives. But you must remember, that absolute power, like most other things which are very bad, is most likely to be broken." Our first President Adams, in his attitude towards this subject, is an example of the sort of statesman, or legislator, described by his wife in one of her later letters: "He who is most strenuous for the rights of the people, when vested with power, is *as* eager after the prerogatives of government."

Mercy Otis Warren, sister of the fiery patriot, James Otis, was a staunch advocate of the "inherent rights" of all the citizens of the new republic. She was the first woman to make use of this celebrated phrase, and to assert that "inherent rights belonged to all mankind, and had been conferred on all by the God of nations." In 1818, Hannah Mather Crocker, grand-daughter of Cotton Mather, published a book, called "Observations on the Rights of Women."* After

* See Appendix A.

this date, and until 1828, there is no record to be found, of any public expression here upon this subject.

In 1828 Frances Wright, an educated English-woman, came to this country to lecture upon the "Moral and Political Questions of the Day, including Woman's Rights." This gifted lady was an able exponent of the doctrines of her eminent country-woman, Mary Wollstonecraft, as set forth in her celebrated book, the "Vindica-tion of the Rights of Woman" Ernestine L. Rose, a beautiful Polish lady, lectured in 1836, in New York and other States, upon the Equal Rights of Women. In 1837, Mary S. Gove spoke upon the same subject, especially upon woman's right to a thorough medical education. About this time Sarah and Angelina Grimké, daughters of a wealthy planter in South Carolina, emancipated their slaves, and came North to lecture on the evils of slavery.

In 1838, Abby Kelley, a young Quakeress, made her first appearance upon the anti-slavery platform. She was the first Massachusetts woman who spoke to mixed audiences of men and women in the State.   As agents of the American Anti-Slavery Society, Abby Kelley and Angelina Grimké went about the State speaking to the people, in school houses and churches, upon the horrors of slavery.   The churches were alarmed at such an innovation, and both men and women were expelled from their body for going to hear them, *especially on Sunday !** Had not St. Paul said that women were to keep silent in the churches ?   It unsexed them, said the church dignitaries, and a Pastoral Letter was written by the General Association of Congregational Ministers in Massachusetts, declaring it to be unnatural that woman should assume the place and tone of man as a public reformer

This "Clerical Bull," as it was called, was ably answered by Sarah Grimké, in a series of letters to Mary S. Parker (President of the

---

*Poor old Abby Folsom deserves some mention, as a martyr to woman's right to speak in public. She was notorious as a "woman's righter," and the boys followed and hooted her along the street. She was one of the first women to speak in anti-slavery meetings. Emerson called her the "Flea of Conventions." But for this impaling on the pen of his genius, her name would have been long ago lost in her forgotten grave.

Boston Female Anti-Slavery Society), and in spite of its interdict, Abby Kelley, and Sarah and Angelina Grimké continued to speak in public, and bring the rights of their sex more and more into the Anti-Slavery Conventions. In the annual report of the American Anti-Slavery Society, for 1839, the question of woman's right to speak upon the platform was endorsed by an "immense majority" in spite of an attempt on the part of some members to "strike out so much as related to the subject" Though women were members of this society, and were permitted to aid in raising money, and in doing a large proportion of the work, they had never been permitted to vote in the conventions, or serve upon its committees.

In the same year a resolution was passed at the annual Convention of the New England Anti-Slavery Society, inviting all persons, whether men or women, who agreed in sentiment on the subject of slavery, to become members and participate in the proceedings. A protest against this resolution was offered, containing reasons why women should *not* be permitted to speak and vote in Conventions; one of which was, that such an "irrelevant innovation" would be "injurious to the cause of the slave." By a strange anomaly, one of the seven signers of this "Protest" against personal liberty was Charles T. Torrey, who was afterwards a martyr to the cause of negro emancipation.

In 1840, woman's right to serve on the board of officers of anti-slavery societies was established, Abby Kelley being put on the business committee of the American Anti-Slavery Society, with the full right to speak and vote upon all questions. This was done in the annual Convention, and some of the members were so exasperated, that a portion of them left the meeting. Of their number were eight clergymen of the same denomination as that which had fulminated the "Clerical Bull." By this event the American Anti-Slavery Society was divided from centre to circumference. But the "Garrisonian wing," as it came afterwards to be called, stood on the right side of the question, and firmly espoused the equal rights of all American citizens, irrespective of sex.

At the World's Anti-Slavery Convention, held in 1840, a similar scene was enacted. The women delegates from America were refused seats in the Convention, and this "insane innovation, this *woman - intruding delusion*," was severely rebuked by the leading English Anti-Slavery members. The men delegates from America, however, sided with the women; George Bradburn, Wendell Phillips, Edmund Quincy, Oliver Johnson, Parker Pillsbury, S. S. Foster, Henry B. Stanton and others, openly protested. Mr. Garrison, who arrived late, refused to take his seat, unless *all* delegates, women as well as men, could be admitted to their rightful privilege.*

These and similar experiences, taught some of the Anti-Slavery people that there was still another class of human beings, besides the black men, who had rights a "white man was bound to respect;" and from that time began the real work for the equal rights of woman. Lydia Maria Child (the first woman journalist in the country), through her able articles in the *National*

* For the World's Anti-Slavery Convention, see Appendix B.

Era, which she edited at that time, began to infuse into the public mind a little leaven of this doctrine.

Abby Kelley never failed, in her speeches upon the Anti-Slavery platform, to make a tacit appeal for the rights of her sex. It was said of her: " She acted like a gentle hero, with her mild decision, and womanly calmness." Angelina and Sarah Grimké, the one with her voice, the other with her pen, eloquently pleaded ; and in the " Garrisonian wing " were many men who helped to sow the seeds of this reform. It is enough to say, that the leaders in the Anti-Slavery movement in Massachusetts were also leaders in the early Woman's Rights movement, and that their voices, if still heard upon the earth, have continued to be identified with the cause.

There were two social influences at work in Massachusetts, in 1840, creating public sentiment concerning this new reform. Leading writers of the time, who belonged to what was then called the Transcendental School, took up the theme. Notable among these was Margaret Fuller, who, in her article entitled " The Great Lawsuit," * struck the key-note of the whole question. She wrote · "We would have every arbitrary barrier thrown down. We would have every path laid open to woman as freely as to man. * * We would have woman lay aside all thoughts such as she habitually cherishes, of being taught and led by men. * * Man cannot by right lay even well-meant restrictions on woman." In her "Woman in the Nineteenth Century," printed two years later, Miss Fuller had advanced to a more practical consideration of the subject. Then she wrote, that man ought to give woman every privilege acquired for himself: elective franchise, tenure of property, liberty to speak in public assemblies, and equal opportunities for education. Theodore Parker, that man of a century; the great Unitarian, Dr. Channing; Ralph Waldo Emerson, William Henry Channing, and A. Bronson Alcott, accepted Miss Fuller's ideas upon this subject.

During the same years in which the *Dial* was published (1840–44), another magazine of a very different literary character, was publishing in a little city not far from Boston. This was the

Lowell Offering, * edited by Harriot F. Curtis and Harriet Farley. Not only was this publication edited, but all its contributions were written by young women, actively employed in the Lowell cotton mills. This was without doubt the first magazine in the country conducted solely by women. It reached a very different class of readers from those of the *Dial,* but it also advocated woman's right to independence of thought and of action. Its influence in Massachusetts and in New England was wide-spread. It found its way into lonely villages and farm-houses, and set the women to thinking, and thus it added its little leaven of progressive thought, to the times in which it lived.

Says Taine: "In order to be developed, an idea must be in harmony with surrounding civilization and the whole age must co-operate with it" It was necessary that the preceding influences, so briefly mentioned, should be at work, in order that the idea of woman's equality with man could become enough developed to demand some public expression on the subject. It had been three

---

* For a history of this Magazine, see Appendix **C.**

2

quarters of a century since the first Massachusetts woman had dared offer a gentle plea for the rights of her sex. The time had come when the voices of many women, in her own and in other states, were to be heard to declare themselves no longer willing to be "bound by any laws in which they had no voice, or representation."

The first Convention to discuss woman's rights and duties was planned by Elizabeth Cady Stanton and Lucretia Mott, and was held at Seneca Falls, New York, on the 19th and 20th of July, 1848. The members of this Convention based the claims of woman on the Declaration of Independence, demanded equal rights, and published their sentiments over their own names. There were present sixty-eight women and thirty-eight men. At the head of the list were the names of James and Lucretia Mott, Elizabeth Cady Stanton, Frederick Douglass (not yet emancipated), Martha C. Wright, and Amy Post. Near the close of the meeting, the members finding that there was still a great deal to be said upon the subject, adjourned for two weeks, and held a similar Convention, in Rochester, New York, on the second of August.

In May, 1850, a third Woman's Rights Convention was held in Salem, Ohio. It was quite well attended and its proceedings were discussed in the columns of the *New York Tribune.*

The first National Woman's Rights Convention was held in Worcester, Massachusetts, October 23 and 24, 1850. This is the fourth convention in order held in the United States to discuss the question of woman's right to equality before the law, to "life, liberty and the pursuit of happiness."

CHAPTER II.

GENERAL HISTORY CONTINUED.   TEN GREAT CONVENTIONS.   1850—1860.

"If there be a word of truth in history, women have been always and still are, over the greater part of the globe, humble companions, playthings, captives, menials and beasts of burden."   MACAULAY.

AT an Anti-Slavery meeting held in Boston in 1850, an invitation was given from the speaker's desk, to all those who felt interested in a plan for a National Woman's Rights Convention, to meet in the ante-room. Nine solitary women responded, and went into the dark and dingy room to consult together. Out of their number a committee of seven was chosen to call a Convention in Massachusetts. The names of this committee were Harriot K. Hunt, Eliza J. Kenney, Lucy Stone, Abby Kelley Foster, Paulina Wright Davis, Dora Taft (Father Taylor's daughter), and Eliza J. Taft. The call was issued, signed by the names of prominent men and women from Massachusetts and different parts of the United States.*

It had been hoped that Margaret Fuller could be prevailed upon to preside at this Convention, and a letter had been written to her, asking **her to** become a leader in the movement, but

"The unplumb'd, salt, estranging sea"

had carried her far beyond the reach of all earthly voices. The Convention was held in Brinley Hall, Worcester, Oct. 23 and 24, 1850, and was called to order by Sarah H. Earle of Worcester, and presided over by Paulina Wright Davis of Rhode Island. Representative men and women were present from the different states, but of the two hundred and sixty-eight names of those who signed themselves members, one hundred and eighty-six were from Massachusetts.

Conspicuous among the speakers were the old Anti-Slavery leaders, Wendell Phillips, William

* For call, and names of members of this Convention, see Appendix D.

Lloyd Garrison, C. C. Burleigh, W. H. Channing and Stephen S. Foster. Among the women who spoke were Abby Kelley Foster, Lucretia Mott, Sojourner Truth, Antoinette L. Brown (whom the newspapers called a "beautiful orthodox Oberlin priestess"), Abby H. Price (the first of those large-hearted women to speak in public on the social question), Harriot K. Hunt (the first Massachusetts woman to protest in public against "taxation without representation"),* Eliza J. Kenney (the first woman whose name had led a petition to the Massachusetts Legislature, asking for the equal rights of her sex), and last but not least, Lucy Stone. This eloquent advocate of woman's rights made her first speech on the subject in 1847. The newspapers of that date said of her: "She is young, has a silvery voice, and a heart warm with enthusiasm." Letters addressed to the Convention were read from Samuel J. May, Elizabeth Cady Stanton, Gerrit Smith and many others.

In the rank and file of the members were also found Anti-Slavery workers, and many others who

* For Dr. Hunt's protest, see Appendix E.

had come long distances to listen, or be converted to the new doctrine of woman's rights and duties. What sacrifices, domestic and social, did not some of these devoted souls make, that they might show the faith that was in them! Many of them are forgotten, and their names have travelled " the way to dusty death," but the flame they helped to kindle, like a " Candlestick set in a low place, has given light as faithfully, where it was needed, as that upon the hill." It is well to keep the " memory green " of those who thus early took up the cross when it was a cross, in this weak, and as it was then often called, ridiculous movement. Their voices sounded the notes of preparation, for the woman's hour that was to be.

Tidings of this and of the Ohio Convention travelled across the ocean, and their deliberations were ably discussed by Mrs. John Stuart Mill, in the *Westminster Review*, and great attention was aroused thereby as to the importance of the subject. It is not too much to say, that the whole Woman's Rights agitation in Old England, as well as in Massachusetts, and in New England, may be dated from these conventions of 1850.

The newspapers of our own State did not follow the lead of the great English Quarterly in its treatment of the new movement, but found this "Hen Convention," as they jocosely called it, a fruitful theme for ridicule. They even went so far as to say that some of the women had voices that sounded like the cackling of hens! So far as known, only four newspapers in Massachusetts treated the subject with sympathy or respect. These were the *Lynn Pioneer*, edited by George Bradburn; the *Liberator*, edited by William Lloyd Garrison; the *Carpet Bag*, a humorous Boston newspaper, whose writers treated the matter sportively but in a kindly spirit, and the *Lowell American*, a little Free Soil newspaper edited and published by William S. Robinson, afterwards so well known in journalism under the *nom de plume* of "Warrington."

Many well remembered anecdotes might be related, to show the drift of opinion of the time, as to the real meaning of this new departure for women. With crude minds the *hen* or *rooster* argument was considered even more conclusive or convincing, than the *sphere* reasoning is to-day.

The central idea of the Woman's Rights movement was supposed to be a desire on the part of
some women to wear men's clothes, and learn to
crow; but whether like men, or like barn-yard
bipeds, was never very clearly defined. When
Lucy Stone went to Malden (a suburban town
near Boston) to speak for the first time for
Woman's Rights, a Universalist clergyman announced the proposed meeting from his pulpit, in
these words: "This evening, at the Town Hall, a
hen will attempt to crow!" This was thought to
be a huge joke!

A second Convention was held in Worcester,
in the same hall as before, on Oct. 15 and 16,
1851. Mrs. Davis again presided, and many of
the speakers and members of the Convention of
1850 were present. The new speakers were
Elizabeth Oakes Smith of New York, Dr. O. Martin, Mehitable Haskell, Charles List and Sarah
Redlon of Massachusetts, Mrs. C. I. H. Nichols
of Vermont, Emma R. Coe of Ohio, Dr. Long-
shore of Philadelphia, and Rebecca Spring of
Brooklyn. Letters were received from Ralph
Waldo Emerson, Henry Ward Beecher, Horace

Mann, Angelina Grimké Weld, Oliver Johnson, Frances D. Gage and others.

Among the letters received from over the ocean was one sent by Jeanne Deroiné and Pauline Roland, two French Socialists, from their prison in St. Lazaré, where they were held in captivity because of their republican principles concerning universal suffrage.* Harriet Martineau also sent a long letter, in which she gave an account of the interest excited in England by the Worcester Convention of 1850, and she also expressed her profound sympathy with the new movement.

It was at this Convention of 1851, that Abby Kelley Foster made the speech containing the little sentence so long and lovingly remembered. She had been urging upon the women their duties, as wives, mothers, and as citizens, and then, in reference to something said by another speaker in disparagement of the Anti-Slavery platform, she, who knew so well what had been done by

* With other reforms, Pauline Roland advocated the doctrine that marriage should never be tolerated, unless the man as well as the woman, could be compelled to keep the law of chastity.

those pioneer workers in order that such a gathering of women could be possible, said, in her inspiring tones : " I do not rise to make a speech ; my life has been my speech. For fourteen years, I have advocated this cause by my daily life. Bloody feet, sisters, have worn smooth the paths by which you come up hither."

A third National Convention was held at Syracuse, New York, in September, 1852. The call was signed bv Elizabeth Cady Stanton, Paulina W. Davis, William H. Channing, Lucy Stone and Samuel j. May. Lucretia Mott presided. The most notable Massachusetts woman who appeared as speaker at this Convention, was Susan B. Anthony. She had been lecturing since 1847, as agent for the temperance cause, but she made her *début* on the Woman's Rights platform at the Syracuse Convention of 1852. Susan B. Anthony's name, with that of Lucy Stone, and Elizabeth Cady Stanton, is known .in connection with the Woman's Rights Movement wherever the English language is spoken or interpreted. For some unexplainable reason, it has been the fortune of these ladies, more than of any other

leaders, to bear the obloquy incident to the movement, and to be considered the typical Woman's
Rights advocates as illustrated in the burlesque
drama, or in caricature. " Susan B." is *par excellence* the martyr to the cause of Woman Suffrage,
since she has been arrested, imprisoned, tried
and convicted on the charge of " voting contrary
to law."

The new speakers, not heretofore mentioned,
were Gerrit Smith, Mr. Howlett, Lydia S. Fow-
ler, Matilda E. J. Gage, Jane Elizabeth Jones,
B. S. Jones, Catherine Stebbins, Ernestine L.
Rose, James Mott, Martha C. Wright, and per-
haps others. Letters of sympathy were read
from Rev. S. J. May, Elizabeth Cady Stanton,
Horace Greeley, Mrs. Hugo Reid of England,
Rev. William H. Channing, John Neal of Maine,
Rev. A. D. Mayo, William Lloyd Garrison, Mar-
garet H. Andrews, Angelina G. Weld, and Sarah
D. Fisk. Mr. C. A. Hammond, of New York
State Committee of the Liberty Party, offered
resolutions of endorsement of the movement.

In 1853 a Woman's Rights Convention was
held at Broadway Tabernacle in New York.

Lucretia Mott presided. Conspicuous among the new names of speakers and workers were those of Rev. John Pierpont, Caroline M. Severance and Rev. John C. Cluer. Madame Anneke, a German lady, editor of a German Woman's Rights paper, addressed the Convention in her own tongue, Mrs. E. L. Rose translating her remarks into English as she spoke.

This Convention is notable from the fact that it witnessed the public confession of one Boston editor, Isaac C. Pray, who, in a spirit of repentance, publicly acknowledged himself converted to the doctrine he had hitherto ridiculed. He said: "This cause has been the butt of all the ridicule I could command. There is not a lady on this platform whom my pen has not assailed; and now I come to make all the reparation in my power, by thus raising my voice in behalf of them and the cause committed to their hands." A praiseworthy example to all Boston editors!*

A letter was read from the Woman's Rights

* This is the only early Convention at which any particular disturbance occurred. According to the records it broke up in confusion. Whether the Boston editor's confession had anything to do with it does not appear.

Association of Illinois, showing the gratifying progress of public opinion on this question in that State. As early as 1853, Indiana, Pennsylvania and others of the States, had begun to follow the good example of New York, Ohio, and Massachusetts, in agitating the new reform.

The same year (1853) a Fourth National Woman's Rights Convention was held in Cleveland, Ohio. Lucretia Mott, the former President of the association, called the meeting to order. Frances D. Gage of Missouri was chosen President, and a fervent prayer was offered by Rev. Antoinette Brown. Massachusetts was represented by Stephen S. and Abby Kelley Foster, Lucy Stone and Wm. Lloyd Garrison. Ernestine L. Rose was chairman of the Business Committee, and Susan B. Anthony of the Finance Committee. William H. Channing, in a letter proposed a Woman's Declaration of Rights, which, with a similar one passed at Seneca Falls, was referred to a committee for final action.

This is not the first time an attempt was made to form a Woman's Declaration of Independence. In a letter from Mr. Francis Cogswell, of Bedford, to E. R. Hoar, President of the Concord (Mass.) celebration of 1850, may be found the following: "In the recent Female Declaration of Independence, framed and signed by the immortal thirty-two ladies of Cambridge, may be found the following significant language: 'We offer,' say the fair rebels, 'as an apology for this our first manifesto, the fact that we have too long been regarded as political cyphers, and that we have sacredly resolved to make the year 1850, memorable as the commencement of a new era in politics.'" This letter was written in April of the same year that the first Woman's Rights Convention was held in Massachusetts. Who the "immortal thirty-two ladies," who framed this document were, has not yet been discovered.

The notable persons who first appeared at the 1853 Woman's Rights Convention, were Joshua R. Giddings ("Old Gid") the great Ohio Free Soil leader, and Henry B. Blackwell. This latter gentleman made a memorable speech upon woman's right to freedom, personal and political. After enumerating the many causes, which led to woman's degradation, he said that even her *dress*, was characteristic of her social condition. And he advised any gentleman present, who did not agree with him as to the cramped condition in which woman was placed, even in the matter of clothing, to try to live one day in her habiliments. In the social position of woman, she found herself still more bound and restrained. Was it any wonder that woman suffered thus fettered and confined from the cradle to the grave? For himself he would not accept life on such conditions.

The Bloomer costume, as it was called, had appeared a few years before, and several leading women — Lucy Stone among them — had adopted the fashion. The credit of originating this costume, afterwards made so famous, belongs to Mrs. E. S. Miller, a daughter of Gerrit Smith of New York. ·She lived in the country near her father's home, and was in the habit of going every day, in all weather, to visit him. Her long dresses were so much of an inconvenience, in walking over the country roads to his residence, that she determined to adopt a costume she had seen Mrs. Fanny Kemble wear on some mountain excursions. She at once proceeded to cut off one of her long dresses just below the knee and with the material thus gained, she made Turkish trowsers, and this, with the addition of a short sack, completed the suit. Afterwards, by one of the caprices of history, this dress, so originated, was named for Mrs. Amelia Bloomer, a lady who also adopted it.

Elizabeth Cady Stanton, Mrs. Miller's cousin, was the second lady to adopt this fashion. Attempts were made to introduce the reform dress generally, among women. Conventions and parlor meetings were held, to discuss the project, and the "Bloomerites" in one city at least, (Lowell), appeared in public, as a part of the Fourth of July procession of 1851, dressed in their unique and striking costume. They were nearly two hundred in number, fair young working girls, from the Lowell Cotton Mills, and if they did not look like "liveried angels," (as they were said to have looked on a similar occasion, when dressed in white, with gay parasols, they walked in procession in honor of Andrew Jackson,) they were a pretty sight, and made a choice subject for the illustrated newspapers of the time. Even the

London *Punch* thought the " American Bloomer-ites " worthy the attention of its artist.   The reform dress though worn several years by leading and progressive women, was finally done to death like many a better fashion, by the ridicule of the newspapers and the boys in the streets.

To return.   In Mr. Blackwell's speech, after he had finished his remarks upon the subject of woman's dress, he endorsed the Bloomer costume and spoke of its peculiarities as follows : " When I first heard about it, it commended itself to my reason, but when I first *saw* it, I confess my taste recoiled from the novelty.   I felt a shock, in spite of myself, as a figure, which seemed neither man nor woman, approached me."   " But," he contin-ued earnestly, " I feel so no longer."   History must tell that he soon passed beyond the *enduring* stage in his conversion, and that a certain little rosy cheeked reformer who wore the "short dress," soon after became to him the dearest woman in the world.

Two years later (1855), Henry B. Blackwell and his wife, Lucy Stone, made their protest against the marriage laws, as then existing, and enunciated their belief, that though married, they were still individuals, with distinct and separate rights ; that woman, as *wife*, could not be absorbed in the *husband*, or extinguished by the marriage ceremony, and that she should still continue to hold her own property, and keep her own name as before marriage. For twenty-five years Lucy Stone and her husband have maintained these opinions.

In 1879, desiring to vote under the new law allowing women to vote for school committees, she applied for registration under her own name, of Lucy Stone. The Registrar of voters gave the opinion that as her married name was Blackwell, her request could not be granted, and the matter being referred to the City Solicitor of Boston, he confirmed this view of the subject.* Not willing to make this concession of principle to an old tradition, Lucy Stone has not yet become a voter.

T. W. Higginson of Massachusetts wrote memorable letters to the 1853 Conventions.

---

* Yet she could not have been registered as Mrs. Henry B. Blackwell ! The question seems to be, which of her husband's names did she marry?

The first Woman's Rights Convention ever held in Boston, was in 1854, at Horticultural Hall, the same day upon which Anthony Burns was carried back into slavery. Though many of the friends staid away to witness this sad surrender, the hall was crowded with earnest men and women, whom a deep interest in the movement had drawn together. The speakers were Lucy Stone, James Freeman Clarke, Harriot K. Hunt, Mr. Phillips, Mr. Garrison, Abby Kelley Foster, William I. Bowditch and many others. Sarah H. Earle of Worcester, presided, and Ellen M. Tarr of Boston, was secretary.

September 19th and 20th, 1855, a New England meeting convened at the Meionaon to consider the laws of the different New England States in relation to women. Harriot K. Hunt presided, and delivered the opening address. Paulina Wright Davis was permanent chairman. Caroline H. Dall reported on the laws of Massachusetts, Mrs. Davis reported from Rhode Island, (this document was drawn up by Dunbar Harris), Ann E. Brown from Vermont, Ellen M. Tarr from New Hampshire, and Francis Gillette from

Connecticut. Caroline M. Severance, Wendell Phillips, Antoinette Brown, T. W. Higginson and Lucy Stone were among the speakers. Ralph Waldo Emerson delivered the closing lecture and Elizabeth Oakes Smith read a poem.

In 1856 the Seventh National Woman's Rights Convention was held in Broadway Tabernacle, New York. Martha C. Wright called the meeting to order; Lucy Stone presided, and made an eloquent opening address. Massachusetts was represented in letters and speakers by Rev. Samuel Johnson, Francis Jackson, T. W. Higginson, A. Bronson Alcott, Susan B. Anthony, N. H. Whiting and Wendell Phillips. Horace Greeley again gave his assurance of sympathy with the cause. He wrote: "If the women of this, or any other country believe their rights would be better secured, and their happiness promoted by the assumption on their part, of the political franchises and responsibilities of men, I, a republican in principle from conviction, shall certainly interpose no objection." * Frances D. Gage, Ernestine

* Mr. Greeley before his death, in 1872, changed his mind upon this subject.

L. Rose and Lucretia Mott also spoke; and Elizabeth Cady Stanton wrote an able letter on woman's rights in the marriage relation.

The 1856 Convention was held just after the election of President Buchanan, a time when the issue of the Anti-Slavery question was the most absorbing thought in the public mind. Fremont had been the candidate of the Republican party, (or "the Party of Freedom,") and the name of Jessie Benton Fremont, had been made a rallying cry of the campaign. The Convention, taking advantage of this fact, made an appeal in its resolutions to both the Democratic and Republican parties to do justice "to both halves of the human race." To the Republican party it said: "Resolved: That the Republican party, appealing constantly, through its orators, to female sympathy, and using for its most popular rallying cry a female name, is peculiarly pledged by consistency, to do justice hereafter in those states where it holds control." It need hardly be added that no notice was taken of this appeal by those to whom it was addressed. And yet the Republican party was fast coming into power, made up of men who were old Anti-Slavery and Free Soil political leaders, whose motto was *Emancipation, Free Speech and a Free World.!*

After Fremont was defeated it seemed to those who had labored so long for the black man's freedom, and for the rights of woman, as if both causes were lost. The Woman Movement was silent for a period of three years, and there is no record of a National or other convention, in which Massachusetts had a part.

A Woman's Rights meeting, the third of the kind in Boston, was held at Mercantile Hall, May 27, 1859, the report of which was published by S. R. Urbino. It was called by Caroline M. Severance and Caroline H. Dall. Mrs. Severance presided and made the address of welcome. Harriot K. Hunt spoke on "Woman: 1st, Restricted in Education; 2d, Deprived of Suffrage; 3d, Taxed without Representation. Rev. James Freeman Clarke, Rev. John T. Sargent, Rev. Charles G. Ames and Wendell Phillips were the speakers. Mrs. Dall made an able report showing what had been the gain to the movement since 1855, in Europe as well as in America.

The Ninth National Convention was held in New York May 12, 1859. A number of the Massachusetts leaders whose names have been mentioned were present, and a committee was appointed to petition the Legislatures of the several states. Their names were, Wendell Phillips, Elizabeth Cady Stanton, Caroline H. Dall, Caroline M. Severance, Ernestine L. Rose, Antoinette B. Blackwell, Thomas W. Higginson and Susan B. Anthony. The Tenth National Convention was held in New York city in 1860, and here nearly the same names are found as workers and speakers.

It will be seen that all the National Conventions, up to this date, though not always held in the State were organized in great part by Massachusetts reformers who had learned so well how to manage them through their Anti-Slavery experience. Hence, some record of the proceedings of the Conventions mentioned, is necessary, in order to make complete the history of the inception of the Woman's Rights Movement in Massachusetts. The hands of her chieftains can plainly be traced holding the leading strings of this great reform. A newspaper correspondent, in the *Springfield. Republican*, writing of this matter, said: "If Boston reformers have not absolutely turned the crank of the Universe for the last thirty years, they have taken a spell at it, perhaps oftener than any other men and women in the country, and deserve to have credit given them accordingly."

CHAPTER III.

GENERAL HISTORY CONTINUED. THE MACHINERY
OF CONVENTIONS. 1860—1881.

" The Ballot is education in Government."
WARRINGTON.

FROM 1860 to 1866 there is no record to be
found, of any public meeting on the subject
of Woman's Rights, in which any Massachusetts
speaker appeared. During these years the war
of the Rebellion had been fought. Pending the
great struggle, the majority of the leaders, who
were also Anti-Slavery leaders, had thought it to
be the wiser policy for the woman cause to give
way for a time, in order that all the working
energy might be given to the cause of the slave.
" It is not the woman's, but the negro's hour."
" After the slave—then the woman," said Wendell
Phillips in his stirring speeches, at this date.

"Keep quiet, work for us," said other of the Anti-Slavery leaders to the women. "Wait! help us to abolish Slavery, and then we will work for you."

And the women, who had the welfare of the country as much at heart as the men, kept quiet; worked in hospital and field; sacrificed sons and husbands; did what is always woman's part in wars between man and man,—and waited. When the Fourteenth Amendment to the United States Constitution was proposed, in which the negro's liberty and his right to the ballot were to be established, an effort was made to secure in it some recognition of the rights of woman. Massachusetts sent a petition, headed with the name of Lydia Maria Child, against the introduction of the word "male" in the proposed new amendment.

When this petition was offered to the greatest of America's emancipation leaders, for presentation to Congress, he received and presented it under protest. He thought the woman question should not be forced at such a time, and the only answer from Congress this "woman intruding" petition received, was found in the Fourteenth Amendment itself, in which the word "male," with unnecessary iteration, was twice repeated, so that there might be no mistake in future concerning woman's rights, under the Constitution of the United States.

The war was over. The rights of the black man, for whom the women had worked and waited, were secured, but under the new amendment (by which his race had been made free) the white women of the United States were more securely held in political slavery. It was time, indeed, to hold conventions and agitate anew the question of woman's rights. The lesson of the war had been well learned. Women had been taught to understand politics, "the Science of Government," and to take an interest in public events; and some who before the war had not thought upon the matter, began to ask themselves why thousands of ignorant *men* should be made voters, and they, or their sex, still kept in bondage under the law.

The "American machinery of conventions," (as our English co-workers call it,) for the Woman's

Rights cause, was set in motion again, May 10, 1866, when the Eleventh National Convention was held in the Church of the Puritans, in New York.

Desiring to stand on a broader platform than that hitherto held. the name of the organization was changed to that of the American Equal Rights Association. Its avowed object was to secure equal rights to all American citizens, "especially the right of suffrage, irrespective of race, color or sex." Elizabeth Cady Stanton was made president of the new named Association. Susan B. Anthony, Lucretia Mott, Ernestine L. Rose, Frances D. Gage, Henry Ward Beecher, Theodore Tilton and others spoke. Massachusetts was represented by Wendell Phillips, Parker Pillsbury, Stephen S. Foster and Caroline H. Dall. Mrs. Dall made an able report on the changes in the social condition of woman, during the interregnum, since her last report at the Convention of 1860.*

It is a notable fact, that at this Convention, the word "Rights," as applied to the Woman Move-

* See Appendix F.

ment, was changed to that of "Suffrage," a Woman Suffrage petition being sent from it to Congress for the first time. But not until 1868–9 did it become the distinctive title of the reform. Since that date, very little has been said about Woman's Rights — but a great deal about Woman Suffrage, or The Suffragists. The latter term is a misnomer, according to the dictionary interpretation, which says, "a suffragist is one who exercises the right of suffrage — a voter."

In 1866 (May 27), the first meeting of the American Equal Rights Association was held at the Meionaon in Boston. Mrs. C. H. Dall called the meeting to order, and Lucretia Mott presided. The speakers were Susan B. Anthony, Dr. Sarah Young, Parker Pillsbury, Aaron M. and Mary Powell, Frances E. Harper, Frederic A. Hinckley, Samuel E. Sewall, Dio Lewis and others. The first anniversary of this Association was held in the Church of the Puritans in New York city, in 1867. On its board of officers were the names of Elizabeth B. Chace, Mary Ashton Livermore, Lucy Stone, Henry B. Blackwell, Susan B. Anthony, Charles L. Remond, Caroline M. Sev-

The American Equal Rights Association lived until 1869, when in Convention, on motion of Ernestine L. Rose, the name was changed to the National Woman Suffrage Association. The same year the present American Woman Suffrage Association was formed. Since that time these two organizations for the same purpose, have continued successful work in different but converging directions. The National is perhaps the more powerful, since its method has been, in great degree, to attack the stronghold of the enemy itself — the Constitution of the United States.

It has been needful, hitherto, to record in part, the suffrage work done in other states, so far as it was projected by Massachusetts leaders, and connected with the work in this Commonwealth. Hereafter the history of the movement will be more confined to work actually done in Massachusetts or in New England.

In November 1868, the call for a New England Convention was issued and the meeting was held on the 18th and 19th of the same month, at Horticultural Hall, in Boston. James Freeman Clarke presided. In this Convention sat many of the distinguished men and women of the New England States, old time workers, together with newer converts to the doctrine, who then and there became forever identified with the cause of equal rights irrespective of sex. John Neal came from Maine; Nathaniel and Armenia White from New Hampshire; Isabella Hooker from Connecticut; Thomas W. Higginson from Rhode Island; and John G. Whittier, Samuel May, Jr., Gilbert Haven, John T. Sargent, Frank W. Bird, Wendell Phillips, William Lloyd Garrison, William S. Robinson, Stephen and Abby Kelley Foster, with a host of others, from Massachusetts, including some of the distinguished writers for the old *Dial.* Lucy Stone and Henry B. Blackwell, who then lived in New Jersey, were also among the speakers.

This was the first of all the *rousing* Conventions held by the Suffragists of the State, and in it many indifferent people were made to see the urgent need for immediate and active work. The writer, (who has since been no backslider) is a living witness of one, who at this time was re-awakened into the spirit of this belief. The hall was crowded with eager listeners anxious to hear what would be said, on a subject thought to be ridiculous by a large majority of people in the community. Some of the women teachers of Boston sent a letter to the Convention, signed with their names, expressing an interest in the suffrage question.

Many good and well remembered speeches were made. Henry Wilson avowed his belief in the equal rights of woman, but thought the time had not yet come for such a consummation, and said that, for this reason he had voted against the question in the United States Senate; "though," he continued, "I was afterwards ashamed of having so voted." Like another celebrated Massachusetts politician, he believed in the principle of the thing, but was "*agin its enforcement.*" This Convention excited a great interest in the community, and in spirit resembled the old Anti-Slavery Conventions. Slavery had long been abolished; and at this date, the Woman Suffrage question began entirely to supersede in popular interest the old Anti-Slavery question. The negro was now no better than anybody else. He had had his day; and it was now the woman's hour.

The New England Woman Suffrage Association was formed at the 1868 Convention. Julia Ward Howe was elected its President, and made her first known address on the subject of woman's equality with man. Because of this action, the women of the country will never cease to honor her. At the right moment, she sacrificed the literary leisure so dear to her; and, in defiance of conventional traditions and usages, came to work upon an unpopular platform, for a weak and doubtful cause. On the executive board were representative names from the six New England states.

By the formation of this Society, a great impetus was given to the Suffrage cause in New England, and in the country. It planned at once a system by which petitions and memorials were sent annually to the different State Legislatures, and to Congress. It asked for, and obtained hearings before these bodies. It held conventions and mass meetings, printed tracts and documents, and put lecturers in the field. It set in motion two Woman Suffrage Bazars, and organized Subscription Festivals, and other enterprises to raise money to carry on the work. It projected the American, and Massachusetts Suffrage Associations; it urged the formation of local and county Suffrage societies, and set up the *Woman's Journal.*

The Hampden County Society was started the same year (1868), with Eliphalet Trask, Frank B. Sanborn and Margaret W. Campbell as leading officers. This was the first county society formed in the State. Julia Ward Howe, a fresh convert of the Convention of 1868, went to Salem to lecture on Woman Suffrage, and the Essex County Society was formed with Mrs. Sarah G. Wilkins and Mrs. Delight R. P. Hewitt (the only two Salem women who went to the 1850 Convention at Worcester), on its executive board. The Middlesex County Society followed, planned by Ada C. Bowles and officered by names well known in that historic old county. The Hampshire and Worcester County Societies brought up the rear; the former planned by Seth Hunt of Northampton, the latter presided over by Rev.

Rush R. Shippen. Local societies were soon after formed in Malden, Lynn, Salem, Taunton, and in numerous other cities and towns.

The New England Association held its first anniversary in May 1869, and the meeting was even more successful than the opening one of the preceding year. On this occasion Mrs. Livermore made her *début* in Boston, as a platform orator. She had spoken the year before, in Springfield, by Mrs. Campbell's invitation, at the formation of the Hampden County Society. ·The newspapers said that this lady spoke even better than she had done at a recent meeting in New York city, and that Mrs. Howe presided with dignity. Such praise from the " Sir Huberts " of the press, meant something in these early days of woman's appearance as orator, or presiding officer.

Many new names came to the front at this date, to give freshness and vigor to the movement. The most important were those of Ednah D. Cheney, Rev. C. A. Bartol, Rev. F. E. Abbott, Rev. Phœbe A. Hanaford and Hon. George F. Hoar. Wendell Phillips and Lucy Stone both spoke at the 1869 Convention, and Gilbert Haven made a masterly argument from the Bible in favor of the equality of the sexes, using the same texts commonly brought forward in favor of woman's subjection to man. It was on this occasion that the "good Bishop," as he afterwards came to be called, was met on leaving the meeting, by one who did not know his opinion on the subject. This person expressed surprise on seeing him at a Woman's Rights meeting, and said: "*What! you* here?" "Yes," said he, "I *am* here! I believe in the thing, and I'm not going to wait to come in at the tag end of this reform. I am going to start in the beginning, and ride with the procession." After this, not until his earthly journey was finished, was his place in "the procession" found vacant.

Since 1869 the New England Association has held its annual meeting in Boston during Anniversary week, (the last week in May), when reports from various states are offered, concerning suffrage work done during the year. The names on the executive board of the New England Association represent some of the best working material of the movement, and at its quarterly meetings, new methods of carrying on the general and local work are often proposed. The latest and most valuable suggestion was made by Rev. F. A. Hinckley, Chairman of the board of 1879-80. Seeing the necessity of making an attempt to circulate in new channels the doctrine of Woman Suffrage, he proposed in his annual report before the Convention, that a new effort be made to reach the people through the public press. Acting upon this suggestion, means were taken to secure the insertion of a weekly article, upon some phase of Woman's Rights, in a leading New England newspaper. The *Sunday Herald* was selected as the one likely to reach the largest variety of readers. The result of this action was that for many successive weeks, articles written by leading women in favor of this cause, were read by men and women in the near and remote cities and villages of New England. It is not easy to estimate the influence upon public opinion of this novel method of presenting the subject.

The American Woman Suffrage Association, a National organization, was started in 1869, by the New England Association. Since its forma-tion, it has held its annual convention in Ohio, New York, Michigan, Pennsylvania, Indiana, Washington, D. C., and in other places.

The call for a Convention to form the Massa-chusetts Woman Suffrage Association, was signed by some of the leading suffragists of the State, with many others, whose names have since added lustre to the movement. The meeting was held in Horticultural Hall in Boston, Jan. 28, 1870. Lucy Stone, M. A. Livermore, S. S. and A. K. Foster, H. B. Blackwell, Rev. W. H. Channing, Rev. J. F. Clarke, Rev. Gilbert Haven, Julia Ward Howe and Elizabeth K. Churchill made eloquent speeches. Susan B. Anthony and Elizabeth Cady Stanton, were among the noted guests from other states.

Mrs. Stanton had the then unprecedented honor of being entertained by the famous Bird Club of Boston at one of its weekly dinners.* On being

* This was long before the era of "Ladies' Night," a pleasant fashion lately introduced by the Papyrus and other gentlemen's clubs of Boston. At the time Mrs. Stanton was the guest of the "Bird Club," even the *Atlantic Monthly* did not include its women writers among the

questioned as to the significance of this unwonted action on the part of the gentlemen diners at the club, one of them remarked, that he was by no means sure that Mrs. Stanton's presence at the dinner indicated any new light on the qnestion of Woman Suffrage, but he added, " I am sure that the company of intelligent ladies is the most pleasant company intelligent men can have, and *vice versa.*"

The Massachusetts Association is the most active of the three Associations named. Its work is generally local, though it has sent help to Colorado, Michigan, and other Western places. For ten years it has kept petitions in circulation, and has presented petitions and memorials to the State Legislatures. It has asked for Hearings and secured able speakers for them. It has held Conventions, Mass Meetings, Fourth of July Celebrations, and in 1873, a Centennial Tea Party. It has helped organize local Woman Suffrage Clubs and Societies, and so far as means

invited guests to the "Contributors' Dinner." May 28, 1881, the "Bird Club" again entertained Mrs. Stanton; also Susan B. Anthony and Harriet H. Robinson.

were found for that purpose, it has printed for circulation Woman Suffrage tracts and kept lecturers in the field. The amount of work done, in agitating and diffusing the subject, by these lecturing agents, can be seen by the statement of Margaret W. Campbell, who alone, as agent of the American, the New England and the Massachusetts Suffrage Associations, travelled in twenty different states and two territories, organizing and speaking for Suffrage Conventions. Mary F. Eastman, Ada C. Bowles, Lorenza Haynes, Elizabeth K. Churchill, Huldah B. Loud, Matilda Hindman and other agents in the lecture field have also done a great deal of missionary work.

The Massachusetts Suffrage Association projected the political movement of 1870, and later, managed all political action except during the existence of a Woman Suffrage State Central Committee. With the latest work of this society might be mentioned its efforts to present before the women of the State in clear and comprehensive form, an explanation of the different sections of the new law "allowing women to vote for school committees." As soon as this law passed

the Legislature of 1879, a circular of instructions to women was carefully prepared by
Samuel E. Sewall, an eminent lawyer and member of the board of the Massachusetts Woman
Suffrage Association, in which all the points of
law in relation to the new right were ably presented. Thousands of this circular of instructions were sent to women all over the State,
and the information contained in it was of so
great value that it was made the basis of all other
"Instructions to Women" upon the subject of
voting under the new law.*

* The last flank movement of the executive board of this
association was directed upon the town meetings of the
State. The law regulating the matter provides that if ten
voters (male) petition the selectmen to insert any article
in the warrant for a town meeting, it then becomes their
legal duty to see that such article is inserted. A sub-com-
mittee of the board having the matter in charge, took
means whereby the following article was introduced into a
great many of the different town warrants, "To see
whether the Town will, by its vote or otherwise, ask the
Legislature to extend to women who are citizens, the right
to bold Town offices and to vote in Town affairs on the
same terms as male citizens." In many towns, this article
was at once dismissed as unworthy of notice or discussion,
but in others warm debates arose, which were worth more to
the cause of Woman's Rights than if favorable action had
been taken. Fourteen towns endorsed the article by a good
majority. Ashby, Leicester, Rockland, Plainfield, Lexington
and Wrentham deserve special mention.

The annual meeting of the Massachusetts Association is held in January. Then reports are presented from the various local societies, and the social, political, and legal phases of the subject of Woman's Rights are ably discussed. The record of conventions and meetings held by the Massachusetts Association by no means includes all similar gatherings held in different towns and cities of the State. The county and local societies have done a vast amount of work in agitating the suffrage cause. For instance, three notable conventions were held by the Middlesex County Society in 1876 * One in Malden, one in Melrose, and one in Concord. This last celebrated town had never before been so favored. The friends of the movement are found in all the Women's Clubs, Temperance Associations, Missionary Movements, Charitable Enterprises and Church Committees. These agencies form a net-work of motive power, which is gradually carrying the reform into all branches of public work.

To close the history of the movement as carried

* For records of these conventions, see Appendix G.

on for thirty years by the machinery of conventions, it will be well to mention the culminating
meeting of the kind, held in Worcester to celebrate the 30th anniversary of the first Massachusetts Woman's Rights Convention. At the annual
Convention of the Massachusetts Association, in
May 1880, the following resolution was passed:

WHEREAS: We believe in keeping the land-
marks and traditions of our movement, and

WHEREAS: It will be thirty years next October,
since the first Woman's Rights meeting was held
in the State, and it seems fitting that there should
be some celebration of the event, therefore

Resolved.: That we will hold a Woman Suffrage
Jubilee, in Worcester, on the 23d and 24th of
October next, to commemorate the anniversary of
our first Convention.

On the committee chosen for this work were
the names of two of the original committee of
1850, Lucy Stone and Abby Kelley Foster.

The Thirtieth Anniversary Convention* was
held in Worcester, October 20th and 21st, 1880,
the same days of the week on which the first Con-

* For particulars of this Convention see Appendix H.

vention was held, and many of the old workers
and friends met once more to congratulate each
other on the results of thirty years of labor.
Rev. William H. Channing, Rev. Samuel May,
Lucy Stone, Mary A. Livermore, Mary F. East-
man, Kate N. Doggett, Rev. F. A. Hinckley,
Ednah D. Cheney, Antoinette Brown Blackwell,
T. Wentworth Higginson, Isabella Beecher
Hooker, Anna Garlin Spencer, Dr. Martha H.
Mowrey and Julia E. Smith Parker made elo-
quent speeches. Harriet H. Robinson read a
condensed history of Massachusetts in the Woman
Suffrage Movement. Interesting letters were
received from Elizabeth Stuart Phelps, F. W.
Bird, H. B. Blackwell, Margaret W. Campbell,
Mrs. C. I. H. Nichols and Frances D. Gage.
Two original Woman Suffrage songs written by
Anna Q. T. Parsons and Caroline A. Mason,
were sung on the occasion.

The news of the death of Lydia Maria Child,
at the age of seventy-eight, which came just as
the Convention went into session, caused both
sorrow and joy in the hearts of those who were
present. Sorrow at the great loss the woman

cause would suffer in her death ; joy, that she had been permitted to see, before leaving this part of her life, the reform for which she had so long labored, advanced so far, and placed so securely, that in the progress of events, there could be for it, no step backward.*

The *Woman's Journal,* the only Woman Suffrage newspaper ever published in Massachusetts, was set up by the New England Association, in

---

* In passing, it may be well to allude to the last Convention of the Massachusetts Woman Suffrage Association held January 27 and 28, 1881, as illustrating the perfection of the American machinery of conventions. The Committee of Arrangements were Mr. S. C. Hopkins, Mrs. J. W. Smith and Mrs. C. P. Nickles. They engaged the twenty-five speakers, appointed the time of speaking, and saw that each one knew his, or her hour, a week beforehand. This was the best and most systematically arranged Convention ever held in Massachusetts. One of the avowed objects of the Convention was to secure the services of new, and if possible young speakers. For this purpose, there were invited a number of persons who had never before been on the Woman Suffrage platform. Among these young speakers were William Ingram Haven, the only son of Bishop Gilbert Haven, and immediately following him, Mrs. Harriette Robinson Shattuck, the elder daughter of "Warrington." It is a noteworthy incident, that these two children, of noble fathers, should have made on the same day, their first speech in the cause of Woman Suffrage. Mr. H. B. Blackwell, in his speech on the same afternoon, made a very happy point of this coincidence.

1869. It was incorporated in 1870, and is owned by a joint stock company, shares being held by leading Suffragists, and Suffrage Associations of New England. Shortly after it was projected, the *Agitator*, then published in Chicago by Mrs. M. A. Livermore, was bought by the New England Association, on condition that that lady should " come to Boston for one year at a reasonable compensation, to assist the cause by her editorial labor, and speaking at Conventions." Lucy Stone and Henry B. Blackwell were invited by the same Society to " return to the work in Massachusetts " and they at once assumed the editorial charge. T. W. Higginson, Julia Ward Howe, and W. L. Garrison were assistant editors. "Warrington," Kate N. Doggett, Samuel E. Sewall, F. B. Sanborn, and many other good writers, lent a helping hand to the new enterprise.

The *Woman's Journal* has been of great value to the cause, and has made the woman movement everywhere better known and appreciated. It has helped individual women, and brought their enterprises into public notice. It has opened its columns to inexperienced writers, and advertised gratuitously, budding speakers. Its able editorials and articles are often widely copied, and in them the news of what the women of the United States are doing, is carried into all parts of the civilized world. Through its columns, the other day was sent intelligence of the fact, that at last, after a century of disfranchisement, the women of New Hampshire, of Massachusetts, of New York and of other states were given their first right to the ballot.

It is hardly necessary to say, that a reform paper is not self-supporting. To sustain the *Woman's Journal* and furnish money for other suffrage work, two mammoth Bazars or Fairs were held in 1870 and in 1871 in Music Hall, Boston. Nearly all the New England States, and many of the towns in Massachusetts were represented by sale-tables in these Bazars ; and as is usual, donations were sent from all directions, and the women worked, as women will work for a cause in which they are interested, to raise money to furnish the sinews of war. Many of them stood day after day behind sale-tables, or worked in the café, as caterers and waiters. Women in whose veins ran some of the best blood of New England, did not hesitate even at that early date to become identified with the Woman Suffrage reform.

The newspapers from day to day were full of descriptions of the splendors of the tables, and the reporters spoke well of the women who had taken this novel method to carry on their movement. People who had never heard of Woman Suffrage before, came, impelled by curiosity, to see what sort of women were those, who thus made a public exhibition of their zeal in this cause. It was a great time to show one's colors on this subject, and to make converts to the new doctrine. It was a great time for meeting and congratulation with co-workers from all over the New England States. In remote places, as well as nearer the scene of action, many people who had never thought of the significance of the Woman's Rights Movement, came to hear of and. consider it, through reading the reports of the Woman Suffrage Bazars.

In closing the general history of the technical work of the Massachusetts Suffragists, it need not be said how actively it has been pushed since the organization of the Association in 1870. It would be difficult to enumerate the conventions held during that time, the names of individual speakers, the number and quality of the speeches made, or the hours upon hours of committee work which has been done. In the little mentioned a great deal must be understood. The names are legion of the workers who have come forward since 1870, and they deserve a chapter by themselves. These earnest men and women, not only as brilliant leaders but also as faithful members of the "rank and the file," have, by being ever ready to act at the right moment, given a lasting impetus to this great reform.

CHAPTER IV.

POLITICAL HISTORY. 1870—1880.

IF birthright, if American democratic ideas, confer the right to vote, or if capacity alone confers it,—either way, the claim of woman is irrefragable; and all there is left, is the debate among the voters, as to whether they will, or how soon they will, yield that mere exercise of forceful authority, which is the only tenure of their superiority in politics, and in government. **" WARRINGTON."**

POLITICAL agitation on the Woman Suffrage question began in Massachusetts early in 1870, and a mass convention was held in Boston to discuss the feasibility of forming a Woman Suffrage political party. Julia Ward Howe presided and Rev. Augusta Chapin offered prayer. The subject was ably discussed by Lucy Stone, Rev. J. T. Sargent, A. Bronson Alcott, H. B. Blackwell, Dr. Mercy B. Jackson, S. S. Foster, Mary A. Livermore, Rev. B. F. Bowles, F. B.

Sanborn, W. S. Robinson (" Warrington "), Gilbert Haven and many others.

The question of a separate nomination for
State officers was carefully considered. Delegates were present from the Labor Reform and
the Prohibitory party, and strong efforts were
made by them to induce the Convention to nomi-
nate Wendell Phillips, who had already accepted
the nomination of these two parties, as candidate
for Governor. The Convention at one time
seemed strongly in favor of this action, the women in particular, thinking that in Wendell
Phillips, they should find a staunch and well
tried leader. But wiser or more politic counsels
prevailed, and it was finally concluded to post-
pone a separate nomination until after the Republican and Democratic conventions had been
held.

A Woman Suffrage State Central Committee
was formed, and began at once active political
work. A memorial was prepared to present to
each of the last-named conventions, and the candidates on the State ticket of the four political

parties of Massachusetts, were questioned by letter concerning their opinions on the right of the women of the State to the ballot. In answer to this letter many of the candidates for State offices of the Republican, the Prohibitory, and the Labor Reform parties responded favorably.

When the Memorial prepared by the State Central Committee was presented to the Democratic State Convention, that body, in response, passed a resolution conceding the *principle* of women's right to suffrage, but at the same time declared itself against its being *enforced,* or put into practice. To finish the brief record of the dealings of the Democratic party, with the Suffragists of the State, and the question of women's rights according to *Democratic* principles, it may as well be said here, that since 1870 it has never responded to the appeals of the Suffragists, nor taken action of importance, in Convention, on this question. The Democratic party has broken no promises to the women, because it has made none. Though a party of the people, as its name implies (in the dictionary), it has hitherto been inconsistently against equal suffrage — or a government " by the people."

At the Republican State Convention held October 5, 1870, the question was fairly launched into politics, by the admission (for the first time) of two women, Lucy Stone and Mary A. Livermore, as regularly accredited delegates. Both ladies were invited to speak, and Mrs. Livermore at the close of her address presented the following memorial :

To the Republican Convention of the State of Massachusetts ·

The undersigned, having been appointed a State Central Committee by *the friends of Woman Suffrage* assembled in Convention at Tremont Temple in Boston, on the 29th day of September, 1870, are instructed by and on behalf of said Convention to lay before your Honorable Body the following

MEMORIAL.

We respectfully represent

That in violation of the *Bill of Rights* of the Commonwealth of Massachusetts, which expressly affirms that "all power resides originally in the People and is derived from them," the women of Massachusetts — one-half of the entire people — are excluded from political power.

That in violation of *the Declaration of Independence*, which declares that "Governments derive their just power from the consent of the governed," all the women of Massachusetts are governed without consent.

That in violation of the fundamental principle of *Representative Government* that "Taxation without Representation is Tyranny," every woman in Massachusetts who is the owner of property is taxed without representation and has no voice in the amount or expenditure of the taxes she is compelled to pay.

We therefore respectfully request that this Convention of the Republican party, which has abolished political distinctions on account of race, color or previous condition of servitude, will declare itself by resolution opposed to political distinctions on account of sex, and in favor of so amending our State Constitution as to extend

suffrage to women on the same terms and qualifications as are prescribed for men.

JULIA WARD HOWE,

JACOB M. MANNING, D. D.

LUCY STONE,

HENRY B. BLACKWELL,

MARGARET W. CAMPBELL,

JESSE H. JONES,

GEORGE H. VIBBERT,

MARY A. LIVERMORE,

WM. G. GORDON,

SETH HUNT,

JAMES FREEMAN CLARKE,

ZILPHA SPOONER,

Woman Suffrage State Central Committee.

The three following resolutions (drawn up by
Henry B. Blackwell) were then offered ·

Resolved, That the Republican party of Massachusetts is mindful of its obligations to the loyal
women of America for their patriotic devotion to
the cause of liberty; that we rejoice in the action
of the recent Legislature in making women
eligible, as officers of the State; that we thank

Governor Claflin for having appointed women to important political trusts ; that we are heartily in favor of the enfranchisement of women, and will hail the day when the educated, intelligent and enlightened conscience of the women of Massachusetts is in direct expression at the ballot box.

Resolved, That there is no logical or reasonable answer to the claim of suffrage and civil equality for women ; that the subject is not to be treated with ridicule or sarcasm, and that when the women of the state or the nation demand equal political rights, those rights must be granted and secured by a constitutional amendment.

Resolved, That the Republican party of Massachusetts, having aided in abolishing political distinctions on account of race, should now, in consistency with its principles, proceed to abolish political distinctions on account of sex, and to establish in the Commonwealth a Government of the people, by the people, and for the people, upon the basis of impartial suffrage for men and women.

The first resolution was presented to the Committee on Resolutions,* who did not agree as to the propriety of reporting it to the Convention, and they instructed their Chairman, George F. Hoar, to state the fact and refer the resolution back to that body for its own action. A warm debate arose, in which several members of the Convention made long remembered speeches on both sides of the question. The resolution was finally defeated, 137 voting in its favor, and 196 voting against it. Although this resolution was defeated the large vote in the affirmative was thought to mean a great deal as a guarantee of the good faith of the Republican party, and the women were willing to remain inactive

* Committee on Resolutions of the Republican Convention of 1870, were:

AT LARGE—Hon. George F. Hoar, Worcester; Robert Johnson, Boston; Hon. Harvey Jewell, Boston; William S. Robinson, Malden.

SUFFOLK—Hon. H. H. Coolidge of Boston. MIDDLESEX—Hon. David H. Mason of Newton. ESSEX—James B. Wildes of Lawrence. HAMPDEN—Hon. A. D. Briggs of Springfield. HAMPSHIRE—Hon. H. G. Knight of Easthampton. PLYMOUTH—Charles G. Davis of Plymouth. BERKSHIRE—Hon. S. Johnson of Adams. FRANKLIN— Lewis Merriam of Greenfield. NORFOLK—Hon. J. M. Churchill of Milton. WORCESTER—Hon. John D. Baldwin of Worcester.

and trust to its promises. It was thought then, as it has been thought since, that most of the friends of Woman Suffrage were in the Republican party, and that the interests of the cause could best be furthered by depending on its action. The women were, however, mistaken, as they have since found out, and they have learned to look upon the famous resolution in its true light. It is now known as the *coup d'état* of the Worcester Convention of 1870, which really got more votes than it was fairly entitled to. After that,— "forewarned, forearmed," said the enemies of the enterprise, and Woman Suffrage planks (or resolutions) have received less and less votes in Republican Conventions.

In 1871 a resolution endorsing Woman Suffrage was passed in the Republican State Convention. In June, 1872, the National Republican Convention at Philadelphia, passed the following: *Resolved:* "The Republican party is mindful of its obligations to the loyal women of America for their noble devotion to the cause of freedom; their admission to wider fields of usefulness is viewed with satisfaction; and the honest demand of any class of citizens for additional rights, should be treated with respectful consideration." The Massachusetts Republican State Convention, following this lead, again passed a Woman Suffrage resolution.*

This was during the campaign of 1872, when Gen. Grant's chance of re-election was thought to be somewhat uncertain, and the Republican women in all parts of the country were called on, to rally to his support. The *National Woman Suffrage Association* had issued "an appeal to the Women of America" asking them to co-operate with the Republican party, to come forward as speakers and writers, and work for the election of its candidates. In response to this appeal, a great ratification meeting was held at Tremont Temple, in Boston, at which hundreds of women

---

*It was as follows:

Resolved: That we heartily approve of the recognition of the rights of Woman contained in the fourteenth clause of the National Republican platform; that the Republican party of Massachusetts as the representative of Liberty and Progress, is in favor of extending Suffrage to all American citizens irrespective of sex, and will hail the day when the educated intellect and enlightened conscience of woman will find direct expression at the ballot box.

stayed to a late hour listening to speeches made by women on the political questions of the day. An address was issued from the "Republican women of Massachusetts to the women of America." In this address they announced their faith in, and willingness to "trust the Republican party and its candidates, as saying what they mean and meaning what they say, and in view of their honorable record we have no fear of betrayal on their part."

During the campaign, Mrs Livermore and Lucy Stone took the stump for Gen. Grant, and women agents employed by the Massachusetts Association were instructed to speak for the Republican party. Women writers furnished articles for the newspapers, and the Republican women on the whole did as much effective work during the campaign as if each one had been a "man and a voter." They did everything but vote! All this agitation and stump speaking did a good thing for the Republican party, but it did a very bad thing for Woman Suffrage, because, for a time, it arrayed other political parties against the movement, and caused it to be thought merely a party issue, while it is too broad a question for such limitation.

General Grant was re-elected and the campaign was over. When the Legislature met and the Woman Suffrage question came up for discussion, that body, composed in large majority of Republican representatives, showed the Republican women of Massachusetts the difference between "saying what you mean and meaning what you say," the Woman Suffrage bill being defeated by a large majority. The women learned by this experience with the Republican party, that nothing is to be expected of a political party as a party, while it is in power, and that the less the Suffragists have to do with the political parties the better, until they conclude to set up for themselves.

To close the subject of suffrage planks, or resolutions in the platform of the Republican party, it may be said that they continued to be put in and seemed to mean something until after 1875, when they became only "glittering generalities," and were as devoid of real meaning or intention as any that were ever passed by the old Whig party on the subject of abolition. After 1872 the suffrage resolutions passed in Republican Conventions were treated, almost invariably, with con- tempt by the representatives chosen by that party to the Legislature; but this same attempt was made year after year, and all the satisfaction the Suffragists got, was what some one called a "new note of hand, of the same amount as the other, never to be paid but still perfectly good—as a note," (like the notes of the recent bogus "Ladies' Deposit Company.")

Yet from 1870 to 1874 the Republican party had the power to fulfil its promises to the Suffragists. Since then it has been too busy trying to keep breath in its own body, to lend a helping hand to any struggling reform. Like the anti- quated barn-yard rooster named "Old Hail the Day," (probably in memory of the resolution of 1872,) it has outlived its usefulness, and can no longer give "a cottage-rousing crow" for freedom. At the Republican Convention held in Worcester in 1880, an attempt was made by H. B. Blackwell to introduce a resolution endorsing the new right conferred upon women, in the recent law allowing women to vote for school committees, passed by the Legislature of 1879. This resolution was.rejected by the committee on that subject, and when offered in Convention as an amendment, it was voted down, without a single voice except that of the mover being raised in its support. Yet this resolution only asked a Republican Convention to endorse an existing right, conferred on the women of the State by a Republican Legislature! A political party as a party of freedom must be very far spent, when it refuses at its annual Convention, to endorse an act passed by a Legislature, the majority of whose members are Representatives elected from its own body.

After the Suffragists as a body had given up all hope of help from the Republican party as a party, after they had seen the futility of questioning candidates and memorializing conventions, and had begun to understand how devoid of intention were the resolutions passed in their conventions, a new departure was determined upon. The question of forming a Woman Suffrage political party had, since 1870, been often discussed. In 1875 Thomas J. Lothrop proposed the formation of a separate organization. But it was not until 1876 that any real effort in this direction was made. The Prohibitory (or Temperance) party sometimes holds the balance of political power in Massachusetts, and many of the members of that party are also strong Suffragists. The feeling had been growing for several years that if forces could be joined with the Prohibitionists, some practical result in politics might be reached, and though there was a difference of opinion on this subject, nearly all the leading Suffragists were willing to see the experiment tried.

The Prohibitory party had at its recent convention in (1876), passed a resolution inviting the women to take part in its primary meetings, with an equal voice and vote in the nomination of candidates and transaction of business. After long and anxious discussions, the Massachusetts Woman Suffrage State Central Committee, in whose hands all political action rested, determined to accept this invitation. A Woman Suffrage Political Convention was held, at which the Prohibitory candidates were endorsed, and a

joint state ticket was decided on, to be headed
" Prohibition and Equal Rights."   These tickets
were sent to Suffragists all over the State, and
the women were invited to go to the polls and
distribute them on election day. Lucy Stone,
Mary A. Livermore· and other leading speakers
agreed to go into the field during the campaign,
and preparations were completed by which it was
expected both parties would act harmoniously together.

Political clubs were formed, at whose head-
quarters during the campaign were seen, night
after night, men and women gathered together to
organize and carry on political work.   From
some window of these head-quarters sometimes
hung a transparency, with " Baker and Eddy "
on one side, and " Prohibition and Equal
Rights" on the other. Caucuses, rallies and
conventions were held in Chelsea, Taunton,
Malden, Lynn, Concord, and other places. A
Middlesex County (First district) Senatorial
Convention was called and organized by women,
and its proceedings were fully reported by the
Boston newspapers.

The nominations made at these caucuses and conventions were generally unanimous, and it seemed at the time as if the two wings of the so called "Baker Party" would work harmoniously together. But with a few honorable exceptions, the Prohibitionists, taking advantage of the fact that the voting power of the women was over, once outside the caucus, repudiated the nominations or held other caucuses, and shut the doors of entrance in the faces of the women who represented either the Suffrage or the Prohibitory party. This was the case invariably, excepting in towns where the majority of the voting members of the Prohibitory party were also Suffragists. This result is what might have been expected, since of what use or importance was this "woman intruding element" in the ranks of *any* political party, with no vote outside the caucus, or at the polls?

After being snubbed in one of their "Prohibitory and Equal Rights" caucuses, the Suffragists, in a town in Middlesex County, determined to hold another caucus. This was accordingly done, and two "straight" Suffrage candidates were nominated as town Representatives to the Legislature. A "Woman Suffrage Ticket" was thereupon printed, to offer to the voters on election day.* The next question was, who would distribute these ballots most effectively at the polls. Some of the men Suffragists thought that the women themselves ought to go to the polls, and present in person the names of their candidates. At first the women who had carried on the campaign work so far shrank from this last test of their faithfulness; but, after carefully considering the matter, they concluded that it was the right thing to do.

The repugnance felt at that time, at the thought of "women going to the polls" can hardly be appreciated to-day. Since the women have begun to vote in Massachusetts, the terror expressed at the idea of such a proceeding has somewhat abated; but in 1876, it was thought to

---

* This "Woman Suffrage Ticket," the first ever offered to a Massachusetts voter, received forty-one votes out of the thirteen hundred and forty cast in all by the voters of the town; a larger proportion than that first cast by the old Liberty party in Massachusetts, which began with only three hundred and seven votes in the whole State, and ended in the Free Soil and Republican party.

be a rash and dreadful act for a woman to appear at the polls, or near the ballot box, in company with the MEN. Some attempt was made to deter these women from their purpose, and horrible stories of pipes and tobacco, and probable insults were told; but they had no terrors to women who knew better than to believe that their townsmen and neighbors would be turned into beasts (like the man in the fairy tale), for this one day in the year.

It cannot be said that some of them did not "quake in their boots" at this unusual proceeding, but they had fortified themselves with brave words, and some of them with prayers and tears, for they were in earnest, and "having done all" were determined to "stand." They stood there distributing votes from nine o'clock A. M., till a quarter of five P. M., only leaving their positions long enough to get a cup of coffee and a lunch, which was provided at the head-quarters.

It was a sight to be remembered, to see women "crowned with honor," pleading with the few colored men who came to the polls, and asking men who were perhaps ten years ago slaves, now that the hour had struck for them, to give their votes to help the women who had so faithfully worked for them when they were in bonds. And so these women stood at the polls and saw the freed slave go by and vote, and the newly-naturalized fellow-citizen, and the blind man, and the paralytic, and the boy of twenty-one, with his newly-fledged vote (HE did not believe in Woman Suffrage), and the drunken man who did not know Hayes from Tilden, and the man who read his ballot upside down. All these voted for the men they wanted to represent them, but the women, being neither colored, nor foreign, nor blind, nor paralytic, nor newly-fledged, nor drunk, nor ignorant, but only *women*, could not vote for the men they wanted to represent them.*

The women learned several things during this campaign in Massachusetts. One was, that weak

* The first time women went to the polls in Massachusetts was in 1870, when forty-two women of Hyde Park, led by Angelina Grimké Weld, and Sarah Grimké, went to the polls on election day, and deposited their ballots, in solemn protest "against the political ostracism of women, against leaving every vital interest of a majority of its citizens to the monopoly of a male minority." It is hardly needful to record that these ballots were not counted.

parties are no more to be trusted than strong ones; and another, that men grant a great deal, but not everything, until the ballot is placed in the hands of those who make the demand upon them. They learned also how political caucuses and conventions are managed. The resolution passed by the Prohibitionists enabled them to do this. So the great "open sesame" is reached. Women have been to petty caucuses, and have remained uncontaminated, and for their escort there and back they must thank the Prohibitory party of 1876. It is but fair to state, that since 1876 the Prohibitory party has treated the Woman Suffrage question with consideration. In its annual convention it has passed resolutions endorsing woman's claims to political equality, and has set the example to other parties, of admitting women delegates to seats in convention. These delegates, however, have been members of the Prohibitory rather than of the Suffrage party.

It will be understood that it is not of individual *members* of the political parties of the State, that the Suffragists have reason to complain; but of the parties themselves, as organized bodies, in their dealings with this question.   In spite of the restrictions of party lines, and the action of their conventions, many members of all the political parties have rendered the cause great service in private, in high official capacity, and as members of the State Legislature.

The result of efforts to mix the question of equal rights for woman with state, or party politics, has been briefly but correctly stated.   The attitude of the dominant political parties is to-day one of perfect indifference.   The weaker ones hold out some inducements to the Suffragists, but how much their resolutions or planks in conventions mean, will be seen when they have grown strong enough to be of real assistance to the cause.   Judging from past experience, it is plainly evident that if any further meddling with politics is to be attempted, a new political party should be formed, having for its basis woman's right to the ballot, which is the only question to justify the formation of such a party, because it is a question of absolute right.   If this cannot be done, the Suffragists must live in the hope that when the political organizations, now so busy in attempting to disintegrate each other have completed the work, out of their best elements will be created a party, whose motto "a pure ballot" will mean what it says, will mean even more than it says, will mean a just ballot for all American citizens.

CHAPTER V.

LEGAL AND LEGISLATIVE HISTORY.

1691—1881.

"Is it only among men that freedom and virtue are to
be united ? Why should the slavery that destroys you, be
considered the only method to preserve us ? It has been
the great error of men, and one that has worked bitterly on
their destinies, that they have made laws unfavorable to
the intellectual development of women. Have they not in
so doing made laws against their children, whom women
are to rear, against the husbands of whom women are to be
the friends, nay—sometimes the advisers ?"

BULWER-LYTTON.

IN the early history of Massachusetts, when
the new colony was governed by laws set
down in the Province Charter, (1691, third year
of William and Mary) women were not excluded
from voting. The clause in the Charter relating
to this matter says: "The Great and General
Court shall consist of the Governor and Council
(or assistants for the time being) and of such

freeholders, as shall be from time to time elected or deputed by the major part of the freeholders and other inhabitants of the respective towns or places, who shall be present at such elections." In the original Constitution (1780) women were excluded from voting except for certain State officers.*

In the Constitutional Convention of 1820, the word "male" was first put into the Constitution of the State, in an amendment to define the qualifications of voters. In this Convention, a motion was made at three different times, during the passage of the act, to strike out the "intruding" word, but the motion was voted down.

There is no evidence that the women ever made use of their voting right, either under the Charter, or under the Constitution; nor is there any proof that they made objection, either singly or in a body, to being thus excluded from the right of franchise. General consent, even of the women themselves, was undoubtedly the origin of the exclusion of women from voting. This was

* For summary of Voting laws relating to women from 1691 to 1822, see Appendix I.

founded, probably, on the supposition that only an infinitesimally small number, if any, would ever want it, and also perhaps on the idea that the women of the country would always be in what was called a domestic sphere. Long before the second attempt was made to revise the Constitution of the State, both these reasons were gone. Large numbers of women began to demand suffrage, and now their sphere of operations and enterprise had become so widened, that they felt they had not only the right, but also an increasing fitness for civil life and government, of which the ballot is but the sign and the symbol.

In the Constitutional Convention of 1853, twelve petitions were presented, from over two thousand adult persons, asking for the recognition of woman's right to the ballot, in the proposed amendments to the Constitution of the State. Abby M. Alcott, wife of the Concord philosopher, and mother of the novelist, Miss Louisa M. Alcott, a woman foremost in the Anti-Slavery reform, asked with other women of Massachusetts, to "be allowed to vote on the amendments that may be made in the Constitution." Francis

Jackson and others asked that the word "male may be stricken from the Constitution." The other petitions were headed by the names of Harriet L. Randall, T. Wentworth Higginson, Wendell Phillips, Josiah Henshaw, Mary Osgood, Mary E. Higginson, J. G. Forman, Betsey T. Heywood, Abby H. Price, and Lucretia Upham. Harriot K. Hunt also petitioned that she might be "allowed to vote, or be excused from paying taxes." All these petitions were referred to the Committee on the Qualifications of Voters, of which Amasa Walker of North Brookfield was the Chairman.

On the petitions of Francis Jackson and Abby M. Alcott the Committee reported leave to withdraw, giving as their reason that, the "consent of the governed" was shown by the small number of petitioners. Hearings before this Committee were granted, and Lucy Stone, Susan B. Anthony, Theodore Parker, Wendell Phillips, and other speakers of learning and ability, presented able arguments in favor of giving women the right to vote. Among the many reasons urged by the petitioners why their petitions should be granted, were the following:

1st. "That women are human beings, and therefore have human rights, one of which is, that of having a voice in the government under which they live, and in the enactment of laws they are bound to obey."

2d. "That women have interests and rights, which are not, in fact, and never will be, sufficiently guarded by governments in which they are not allowed any political influence."

3d. "That they are taxed, and therefore, since taxation and the right of representation are admitted to be inseparable, they have a right to be represented."

A summary of the reasons given was included in the Committee's report. The Chairman of this Committee in presenting this report, moved that all debate on the subject should cease in thirty minutes, and on motion of Benjamin F. Butler of Lowell, the whole report, excepting the last clause, was stricken out. There was then left of the whole document, (including more than two closely-printed pages of reasoning) only this,—"it is inexpedient for this Convention to take any action in relation thereto." The vote was then taken, and woman's right to the ballot in the proposed amendments to the Constitution of Massachusetts, was voted down, 108 to 44. A quick disposal of a mighty subject!

Edward L. Keyes of Abington, and William B. Greene of North Brookfield were the Woman's Rights champions in the Constitutional Convention of 1853. Lucy Stone's axiom, that " women are classed politically with criminals and felons," finds confirmation in one of the decisions of the Committee on the Qualifications of Voters, since it reported in one and the same bill, *inexpedient to legislate* on excluding "from the right of suffrage, and the right to hold any office of profit or trust, all persons who may be convicted of bribery, larceny or other infamous crime ;" . . . *also*, on the petition of Harriot K. Hunt that she may be "excused from paying taxes, or be allowed to vote."

It is a significant fact, that, when the amendments proposed by the Constitutional Convention of 1853 came before the voters of the State, for their sanction by ballot, they were all defeated.

The labor of that august body thus went for nothing, and the money it cost the State, money furnished partly by the taxes of the unrepresented portion of its citizens, was all thrown away! A prophet might have said, that it was not yet time for Massachusetts to change, or amend its Constitution, particularly that part which relates to the "Qualifications of Voters." The year 1880 was the centennial year of the Constitution, and would have been a fitting time to renew the attempt to amend this document, which, though very nearly right in principle, fails in the application of those principles to the political rights of the majority of the people whom it governs.

Legislative agitation on the Woman's Rights question, began in 1849, when William Lloyd Garrison presented the first petition on the subject to the State Legislature.* Before this time, that body had not recognized the word "woman"

---

* Following Mr. Garrison's petition was one from Jonathan Drake and others, "for a peaceable secession of Massachusetts from the Union." Both these petitions were probably considered by the Legislature to which they were addressed as of equally incendiary character, since they both had "leave to withdraw" in company.

enough to admit it into the record of its proceed-ings. In looking over the Index of the Journal of the House, for many years previous to 1851, there is found no mention of legislation for wo-man, either as maid, wife. or widow. In 1851, an Order was introduced asking "whether any legislation was necessary concerning the wills of married women?" In 1853 a bill was enacted "to exempt certain property of widows and un-married women from taxation."

Not until eight years after (in 1861) does the word "woman" appear in the Index of the Jour-nal of the House. That year the Legislature debated a bill to allow a widow, "if she have woodland as a part of her dower, the privilege of cutting wood enough for one fire." This bill was defeated, and the widow, by law, was *not* allowed to keep herself warm with fuel from her own wood-lot. In 1863 the word "wife" first appears in the House records, and legislation began concerning her legal status. A bill asking that "a wife may be allowed to be a witness and proceed against her husband for desertion," was reported inexpedient, and a bill was passed to *prevent* women from forming co-partnerships in business.

In 1865, our lamented Gov. Andrew, seeing the magnitude of the approaching woman question, tried his hand at disposing of one phase of the subject. In his annual message to the Legislature, he made a memorable suggestion with regard to a portion of the citizens of Massachusetts. Said he: "I know of no more useful object to which the Commonwealth can lend its aid, than that of a movement, adopted in a practical way to open the door of emigration to young women, who are wanted for teachers, and for every other appropriate, as well as domestic, employment in the remote West, but who are leading anxious and aimless lives in New England." By the "anxious and aimless" it was supposed the Governor meant the widowed, single, or otherwise unrepresented portion of the citizens of the State.

No action was taken by the Legislature upon this portion of the Governor's message. But a member of the Senate actually made the following proposition before that body, namely,—"That the 'anxious and aimless women' of the State should assemble on the Common on a certain day of the year, (to be hereafter named) and that Western men who wanted wives, should be invited to come here and select them." Legislators who make such propositions, do not foresee that the time may come, when, perhaps those nearest and dearest to them, may be classed among the superfluous, or "anxious and aimless" women!

In 1865 the expediency of allowing married women to testify in suits at law where their husbands are parties, was considered, and an order permitting them to hold trust estates was rejected. It will be seen that though all this legislation was adverse to woman's interest, the question had obtained an entrance into legislative halls, and had forced itself upon the attention of the members of both House and Senate.

In 1866 a joint committee of both Houses was appointed, to consider "if any additional legislation can be adopted, whereby the means of obtaining a livelihood by the women of this Commonwealth may be increased, and a more equal and just compensation be allowed for labor."

In 1867 Francis W. Bird presented the petition of Mehitable Haskell of Gloucester for "an amendment to the Constitution extending suffrage to women." In 1868 Mr. King of Boston presented the same petition, and it was at this time, and in answer to this petition, that the subject first entered into the regular Orders of the Day, and became a part of the official business of the House of Representatives.* When this position is once secured for a question, (whether petitions are presented on the subject or not) it must appear in some form, in the annual record of legislative business, until it is decided one way or the other.

Attempts to legislate on the property question concerning married women were continued in 1868 in bills "to further protect the property of married women," "to allow married women to contract for necessaries," and if "divorced from bed and board, to allow them to dispose of their own property." These bills were all defeated.

*This was brought about through the special efforts of Hon. Francis W. Bird, a member, and W. S. Robinson, ("Warrington,") Clerk of the House of Representatives in 1868.

Annual legislative hearings on Woman Suffrage began in 1869. These were first secured through the efforts of the executive committee of the New England Woman Suffrage Association. Eight thousand women had petitioned the Legislature that suffrage might be allowed them on the same terms as men, and in answer, two hearings were held in the Green Room at the State House. The Committee were addressed by Wendell Phillips, Julia Ward Howe, Lucv Stone, Rev. James Freeman Clarke, Hon. George F. Hoar, and others.*

A remonstrance was also sent into the Legislature, from two hundred women of Lancaster, Massachusetts. The following were among the reasons given why women should *not* be allowed to vote · "The exercise of the elective franchise would diminish the purity, the dignity and the moral influence of woman, and bring into the family circle a dangerous element of discord." It did not occur to these women that by thus remonstrating they were doing just what they were protesting against.

For early legislative hearings, see Appendix J.

What *is* a vote? An expression of opinion, or a desire as to governmental affairs, in the shape of a ballot. The "aspiring blood of Lancaster," should have mounted higher than this, since, if it really was the opinion of these remonstrants that woman cannot vote without becoming defiled, they should have kept themselves out of the Legislature, should have kept their hands from petitioning, and their thoughts from agitation on either side of the subject. Just such illogical reasoning on the Woman Suffrage question, is often brought forward, and passes for the profoundest wisdom and discreetest delicacy!

In 1870 a joint special Committee on Woman Suffrage was formed, and since that time there have been one or more annual hearings on the question, before the gentlemen composing that body. These gentlemen usually are good types of the enlightenment and ability of the Massachusetts Legislature, and they have patiently and respectfully listened to the arguments of the earnest men and women who have come before them asking for changes in the laws, which shall secure to woman equality and the rights of citizenship. To what extent legislative sentiment has been created is shown in the improvement in the laws, with regard to the legal status of woman.

William Claflin was the first governor of Massachusetts to present officially to the voters of the Commonwealth the subject of woman's rights as a citizen. In his address to the Legislature of 1871, he strongly recommended a change in the laws regarding suffrage and the property rights of woman. His attitude towards this reform made an era in the history of the executive department of the State. Legislation then began in earnest, and the subject was forever lifted out of the limbo of legislative contempt.*

Since 1871 nearly every governor of the State has, in his annual message, recommended the subject to respectful consideration. In 1879 Governor Thomas Talbot proposed a constitutional amendment which should secure the ballot to women on the same terms as men. In response to this portion of the Governor's message, and to

* Two years before, (1869) a lady, sitting as visitor in the gallery of the House of Representatives, heard the whole subject of woman's rights referred to the (bogus) Committee on Graveyards!

the 98 petitions presented on the subject, a general Suffrage Bill passed the Senate by a two-thirds majority, and an Act to "give women the right to vote for members of School Committees," passed both branches of the Legislature and became a law of the State.*

In finishing the record of official action on the part of the governors of the State up to the present time, it will be well to record that John D. Long, in his inaugural address before the Legislature of 1881, expressed his opinion in favor of Woman Suffrage perhaps more decidedly than any who had preceded him in that high official position. What he said is worthy to be quoted in full:

"I believe that the State is made more secure in proportion as every member of it of mature age and sound mind has a voice in its administration, and that no one class anywhere can be

---

* This law was run through the legislative wringer in March, 1881, and a part of its absurdity was squeezed out of it. As amended, it may now pass for a very fair law— as a School Committee Suffrage Law. But it is still nothing but a crumb of comfort from the loaf for which the believers in Equal Rights have so long hungered.

safely intrusted with the irresponsible keeping of the rights of any other. The restrictions on suffrage and upon the right of each citizen to cast one vote and have it counted, should, therefore, be as light, and the safeguards of that right as strong, as possible. It is for this reason, as well as because suffrage is a right and not a grace, that, in my judgment, women, paying taxes as they do, and with their personal interests and property subject to legislation, should secure by an amendment to the Constitution the right to vote, and thereby have a voice in the imposition of taxes upon their property, and in the making of laws that affect their lives, liberty and happiness."

The law allowing women to vote for School Committee is one of the last results of the legislative agitations of the Suffragists, though it is true that the petition, the answer to which was the passage of this act, did not emanate from them.* In view of the numerous petitions with

---

* The petition for School Suffrage was the outcome of a conference on the subject, held in the parlors of the New England Women's Club, and was perhaps intended to serve

which the Massachusetts Suffragists have flooded the Legislature during the last 30 years, it is a singular fact, that with this one they had nothing directly to do, though it is none the less certain that without their continued agitation, the passage of the act at this time would not have been possible.

But the petitions of the Suffragists had always been for general and unrestricted suffrage, as Mr. Garrison would say for "*immediate and unconditional emancipation,*" and they had always opposed any scheme for securing the ballot on a class or a restricted basis. They had never been led astray by any such semblance of reform, holding that the true ground of principle is, *equality of rights with man,* and that humanity is a unit: one glory and one shame.

The practical result so far of voting for School Committee has justified this position held by the Suffragists of Massachusetts. For, as shown

as a means of re-instating Abby W. May and other women who had been defeated as candidates for re-election on the Boston School Board. The names of Isa E. Gray, Mrs. C. B. Richmond, Elizabeth P. Peabody, and John M. Forbes led the lists of petitioners.

by the recent elections, the women of the State have not availed themselves to any extent of their new right to vote, and therefore, the measure has not forwarded the cause of general suffrage. In point of fact the law allowing women to vote for School Committee * is a class suffrage law, because under its provisions (according to the general interpretation) the rich, or property tax-paying woman can vote without paying an additional poll-tax; but the poor, or non-property holding woman, must pay a poll-tax of two dollars, or a little less perhaps, if the law is interpreted favorably in her case.

The poor women voters in the State have been quick to see the injustice of being required to pay for this fiction of a right, (which the rich women get for nothing) the same amount of money which men pay for every right the government grants. To such women, except in some local emergency, the privilege of merely voting for school committee is not worth the money it costs. "Does it pay?" is a question the female members of the family can answer, quite as well as the

* For this law see Appendix K.

male members. If the law were really a "School Suffrage Law" and included the question of school appropriations, school supervisors, or management, the building of enormous and costly school houses, or even concerning the books their children were to use, the result might be different, and the women might become enough interested to pay the hard earned two dollar poll-tax for the new privilege. But for School Committee, alone, "No I thank you!"

In fact the School Committee question is not a vital one with either male or female voters, and it is impossible to get up any enthusiasm on the subject. As a test question, upon which to try the desire of the women of the State to become voters, it is a palpable sham. As a sop to those who do not believe in "taxation without representation" it is a miserable subterfuge. Our revolutionary fathers would not have fought, bled and died for such a figment of a right as this; and their daughters, or granddaughters, inherit the same spirit, and if they vote at all, want something worth voting for.

The tax-paying women seem to care no more

for the new privilege than those who are required to pay for it, and even those women who do not believe in "Woman Suffrage" but who do believe in "School Suffrage" have not to any extent been lured from their homes to vote upon this so called important question.

The result is, that the voting has been largely done by those women who have long been Suffragists, and who have gone to the polls on election day, from pure principle, and a sense of duty, rather than from any desire to vote upon such an insignificant matter. The number of women who have voted in the State, is not so much a fair representation of those who desire to vote, as it is a fair representation of the Woman Suffragists who have voted.*

By a careful examination of the law allowing women to vote for School Committees, it will be seen that it is very elastic and capable of many readings, or interpretations. Indeed, it reminds

---

*At the first annual election for School Committee in cities and towns in 1879–80, about 5,000 women became registered voters. Harriette R. Shattuck (the daughter of "Warrington") was the first woman in Massachusetts to express publicly her desire to vote under the new law.

one of the old school exercise in transposing
the famous line in Gray's Elegy ·

"The ploughman homeward plods his weary way,"

which has been found to be capable of over
twenty different transpositions. The collectors
and registrars in towns and cities have taken
advantage of this obscurity of expression, and
interpreted the law according to their individual
opinion on the Woman Suffrage question itself.
In places where these officials have been in sympathy, a broad construction has been put upon
the provisions of the law, the poll-tax payers
have been allowed to vote, upon the payment of
one dollar (under the divided tax law of 1879),
and the women voters generally have been given
all necessary information, and treated courteously
both by the assessors and registrars and at the
polls.

In places where leading officials were opposed
to women's voting, the case has been far different.
Without regarding the clause in the law which
says that a woman may vote upon paying either
State *or* County poll-tax, such officials have

threatened the women with arrest, when they refused to pay both State *and* County poll-tax. In some towns the women have been snubbed and treated with great indignity, as if they were doing an unlawful or a disgraceful thing.

In one town the women voters were actually required to pay a poll-tax the second year, in spite of the clause in the law which says that a female citizen who has paid a State or County tax within two years shall have the right to vote. The town assessor whose duty it was to inform the women voters on this point of the law, when asked concerning the matter, *willfully* withheld the desired information, saying he "did not know," though he afterwards said that he *did* know but intended to let the women "find out for themselves," or words to that effect. This Assessor forgot that the women, as legal voters, had a right to ask for this information, and that by virtue of his official position he was legally obliged to answer.

The law allowing women to vote for School Committees with all its defects and contradictions is not responsible for blunders of this sort, since in all its provisions, the most obtuse intellect cannot fail to find this one interpretation, namely: That it is a law of the State, made in good faith by a majority of the Legislature of 1879, and is a virtual acknowledgment of woman's right to the ballot,—that keystone of American institutions. It is to be regretted, however, that a better test question than that of School Committee Suffrage, could not have been given to the women of the State, so that the issue of what under the circumstances cannot be called a fair trial of their desire to vote, might be more nearly what the friends of the reform had desired.

A School Suffrage Association was formed in 1880, and held its first annual meeting in anniversary week, at Freeman Place chapel. Abby W. May of Boston was elected President, and Ednah D. Cheney, Mary F. Eastman, Anna Garlin Spencer, and other prominent women, not all of them Suffragists, were put upon its executive board.

The first petition to the Massachusetts Legislature, asking that women might be allowed to serve on school boards was presented in 1866 by Samuel E. Sewall of Boston. The same petition was again presented in 1867. About this time Ashfield and Monroe, two of the smallest towns in the State, elected women as members of the School Committee. Worcester and Lynn soon followed the good example, and in 1874, Boston, for the first time, chose three women to serve in this capacity.* There had hitherto been no open objection to this innovation, but the School Committee of Boston not liking the idea of women co-workers, declared them ineligible to hold such office.

One of the women elect, (Miss Peabody) applied to the Supreme Court for its opinion upon the matter, but the judges refused to answer, and dismissed the petition on the ground that the School Committee itself had power to decide the question of the qualification of members of the board. The subject was brought before the Legislature of the same year, and that body, almost unanimously, passed " an Act to declare women eligible to serve as members of School Com-

---

* Their names were Lucretia P. Hale, Abby W. May, and Lucia M. Peabody.

mittees." Thus the women members were reinstated.*

This refusal on the part of the Supreme Judicial Court of Massachusetts to answer a question relating to woman's rights under the law, was received with .a knowing smile by those who remembered the three decisions relating to women which had been given by that august body. The first of these decisions was on the case of Sarah E. Wall of Worcester. The second was concerning a clause in the will of Francis Jackson of Boston, who left $5,000 and other property to the woman's rights cause, the money to be used for lectures and documents, and to secure the passage of laws granting women, whether married or unmarried, the right to vote, hold office, manage property, and enjoy civil rights. The will was

---

* This Act, so brief and so *expressive*, is worthy to be remembered. It simply reads: "*Be it enacted, etc., as follows:*

Sect. 1. No person shall be deemed ineligible to serve upon a School Committee by reason of sex.

Sect. 2. This Act shall take effect upon its passage. (*Approved June* 30, 1874.)"

By force of habit, the Legislature said not a word in the law about *women*.

contested by some of Mr. Jackson's heirs; the Supreme Judicial Court was appealed to, and it decided (in 1867) that anything concerning woman's rights did not constitute a legal charity, and therefore was inoperative and void.

Its third adverse decision* was given in 1871. In that year, Mrs. Julia Ward Howe and Miss Mary E. Stevens were appointed be Governor Claflin as Justices of the Peace. Some member of the Governor's Council having doubted whether women could legally hold the office, the opinion of the Supreme Court was asked and it decided substantially that because women were women, or because women were not *men*, they could *not* be Justices of the Peace; and the appointment of the women Justices of the Peace was not con-firmed. Samuel E. Sewall and other gentlemen of legal minds dissented from this opinion, and the ridicule thrown upon this " Court of high appeal " warned the Judges that it would not do to be caught napping again. Hence, as before stated, when appealed to for the third time to settle a question relating to the legal status of the women

* For these decisions, see Appendix L.

citizens of the State, the Bench refused to answer.

The result of legislative agitation on the Woman's Rights question, is faithfully told in the admirable pamphlets of Samuel E. Sewall* and William I. Bowditch.† Thirty years ago, when the Woman's Rights Movement began, the status of a married woman was little better than that of a domestic servant. By the English common law, her husband was her lord and master. He had the sole custody of her person, and of her minor children. He could "punish her with a stick no bigger than his thumb," and she could not complain against him.

The common law of this state held man and wife to be one person, but that person was the husband. He could by will deprive her of every part of his property, and also of what had been her own before marriage. He was the owner of all her real estate and of her earnings. The wife could make no contract and no will, nor without her husband's consent dispose of the legal inter-

* "Legal Condition of Women in Massachusetts."

† "Taxation of Women in Massachusetts," and "Woman Suffrage a Right, not a Privilege."

est of her real estate. He had the income of her real estate till she died, and if they ever had a living child his ownership of the real estate continued till his death. He could forbid her to buy a loaf of bread or a pound of sugar, or contract for a load of wood to keep the family warm. She did not own a rag of her own clothing. She had no personal rights, and could hardly call her soul her own.

Her husband could steal her children, rob her of her clothing and her earnings, neglect to support the family; and she had no legal redress. If a wife earned money by her labor, the husband could claim the pay as his share of the proceeding. A woman, either married or unmarried, could not hold property, except through trustees. She could hold no office of trust or power. She was not a person. She was not recognized as a citizen. She was not a factor in the human family. She was not a unit; but a zero, a nothing, in the sum of civilization.

To-day, a married woman can hold her own property, if it is held or bought in her own name, and can make a will disposing of it. A man is no longer the only heir of his wife's property. A married woman can now make contracts, enter into co-partnerships, carry on business, invest her own earnings for her own use and behoof,—and she is also responsible for her own debts. She can be executrix, administratrix, guardian or trustee. She can testify in the courts for or against her husband.

If a husband sees fit to whip his wife with a "stick no bigger than his thumb" she can have him bound over to keep the peace for two years. If she lives apart from him she can attach his property for the support of herself and her children. She can release, transfer, or convey, any interest she may have in real estate, subject only to the life interest which the husband may have at her death. A married woman is now the owner of her own clothing to the value of $2,000, although the act granting this (passed in 1879) calls such apparel the "gifts of her husband," not recognizing the fact that most married women earn or help to earn their own clothes.

There is a certain clause sometimes found in old wills, to the effect that if a widow sees fit to marry again, she shall forfeit all right to her husband's property. The most conservative judge in the Commonwealth would now rule that a widow cannot be kept from her thirds, or fair share of the property, by any such unjust restriction. In a husband's eyes of a hundred and fifty years ago, a woman's mission was accomplished after she had been *his* wife and borne *his* children. What more could be desired by her, he argued, but a corner somewhere in which, respectably dressed as his *relict* (or leavings), she could sit down (in the Miss Haversham style) and mourn for him, for the rest of her life.*

The law no longer sanctions the making of such a will, but provides that the widow shall have a fair share of all personal property. A husband can no longer make a will leaving his wife a mere "incumbrance" to his estate, to be toted round, an unwelcome guest, from house to

---

* In an old will (made a hundred and fifty years ago) a husband of large means bequeathed to his "dearly beloved wife" $50 and a new suit of clothes, with the injunction that she should return to her original, or family home. And with this small sum, as her share of his property, he returned her to her parents.

house of relatives or children. If a widow permits herself to-day to be defrauded of her legal rights, in the division of property, it is her own fault, and because she does not study and understand for herself the General Statutes of Massachusetts, and the laws concerning the rights of married women.*

The result of thirty years of property legislation for women is well stated by Mr. Sewall in his admirable pamphlet, in which he says, "the last thirty years have done more to improve the law for married women, than the four hundred preceding." The Legislature has, during this time, enacted laws allowing women to vote in Parishes and Religious Societies; declaring that women *must* become members of the Board of Trustees of the three State Primary and Reform Schools, of the State Workhouse, of the State Almshouse at Tewksbury, and of the Board of Prison Commissioners; also that certain officers and managers of the Reformatory Prison for Women at Sherborn, "shall be women." Without legislation, women now are School Super-

* See Bishop on the Law of Married Women.

visors, Overseers of the Poor, Trustees of Public Libraries and members of the State Board of Education and of the State Board of Health, Lunacy and Charity.

The great changes in the legal and legislative condition of the women of Massachusetts are the direct result of the labors of the Suffragists. By conventions and documents they have informed the people and enlightened public sentiment. By their continued agitation the question has been kept prominently before the voters of the state, and before their representatives in the Legislature. And though so much has been gained, the Suffragists are still hard at work, nor will they rest from their labors, until, both legally and politically, woman's equality with man before the law is firmly established.

The little actual gain in votes since 1870, in favor of municipal or general suffrage for women, might cause the careless observer to draw the inference that no great progress had been made in legislative sentiment during all these years.*

* In 1870 the vote in the House of Representatives on the General Woman Suffrage Bill was as follows; yeas 68,

But those who have carefully noted the expression of the House, year after year, can see a marked change in its attitude towards this subject. It is this: the opposition is at last silenced. The arguments against woman's right to the ballot are all exhausted, or have been refuted, and the opponents have been driven to entrench themselves behind an unreasoning " no."

On March 29th, 1881, the Bill in favor of Municipal Suffrage to Women came before the House for final action, and was ably supported by Col. T. W. Higginson, Cambridge, William Johnson, Everett, G. A. Shepard, Sandisfield, E. P. Brown, Boston, and James F. Almy, Salem. Nearly every member was in his seat, and the opponents were there in full force, ready to vote; but not a voice was raised against the Bill, though Mr Brown of Boston (in his speech) called on the young lawyers and others known to be its enemies, to show their colors and speak for their side of the question. It is safe to predict that so far

nays 133. In 1881 the Bill giving Municipal Suffrage to women was defeated in the House by a vote of 122 nays to 76 yeas.

as speech-making is concerned, legislative opposition to woman suffrage is at last silenced.

It was enough to make the women who sat in
the gallery weep, to hear the "O's" and the
"Mc's," almost to a man, belch forth the em-
phatic "no;" and to think that these men (some
of whom a few years ago were walking over their
native bogs, with hardly the right to live and
breathe), should vote away so thoughtlessly the
rights of the women of the country in which they
have found a shelter and a home. Some of them
must be men who have done nothing to entitle
them to the right of suffrage. When they came
to this country, poor, and with no inheritance but
the "shillalah," the ballot was freely given to
them, as the poor man's weapon for defence.
Why cannot men, who have been political serfs
in their own country, see the incongruity, the
wickedness, of what they do when they cast their
vote against the enfranchisement of over one-half
of the inhabitants of the State which has made
free human beings of them?

If it was a sad sight to the women spectators
to hear their adopted countrymen vote their

rights away, it was enough to make angels weep to hear the dogged "No" come from the lips of men in whose veins runs a thin stream of that blood once famous in the annals of personal liberty. Far better that their revered names should never be heard of again, than that they should be found with those who vote against the rights of the people.

A certain newspaper said, that after the defeat, the women who had been sitting in the gallery went smiling home, feeling quite relieved, and glad to know that their Suffrage Bill was not carried : for, if it had been, they would have had nothing more to fight for. If any of the women "smiled," it was with grim irony to see the men who represent the "blue blood" of Massachusetts join forces with the immigrant and the foreigner, to prevent the women of their own class from enjoying the rights of citizenship. This thought was enough to have made the emblematical stuffed codfish smile, and the Indian in bas relief on the Massachusetts coat of arms, get down from his honored place over the Speaker's desk, and flee from his native State to find a home in a new reservation far beyond that of the persecuted Poncas.

The change in legislative sentiment on the woman suffrage question, can best be illustrated (as Abraham Lincoln would have said) "by a little story" of a conjugal scene.

Mary and John have been married several years. One day Mary makes up her mind that she wants a new and expensive dress; and since she has never any money of her own, she is, of course, obliged to ask her husband to give her the needful sum, and the following conversation ensues:

Mary. John, I want some money to buy a new silk dress.

John. What do you want of another dress? You've got all you need. You said the other day you had more clothes than you wanted.

Mary. Oh! When I said that, I meant the sort of clothes you sometimes buy for me,—that yellow-sprigged calico, for instance, and that great staring shawl — not the kind I pick out to suit myself.

John. It's perfect nonsense for you to get

more dresses. You've got as many again as your mother ever had. It's perfectly ridiculous.

Mary persists, and continues to tease for the dress, until John finally throws down a little money, and leaves the house. When he comes home at night, feeling good-natured, he says· "Well, how does the new dress you *picked. out yourself* suit you?"

Mary. I did not have half money enough to get what I wanted.

John. Not money enough?· Why, I gave you all you asked for!

Mary. Well, there wasn't half enough. No woman could buy a decent dress with such a little—

Here John fires up, and says:

"Well, you shan't have any more. I gave you enough for any reasonable woman. You won't know how to use it if I give you any more, and you shan't have another cent."

In spite of this decision of John's, Mary does not take "no" for an answer, and day after day renews the attack, until John, tired out with her importuning, is finally caught in a yielding mood,

"There, do take all the money you want!"

The parallel is, that in the beginning the Massachusetts Legislature ridiculed the idea of woman suffrage, then it yielded, and gave a little school committee suffrage. Now, in 1881, it is in the dogged, or "you shan't have it" stage. By and by, when it has been importuned long enough, it will say to the women ·

"There, do take all the *suffrage* you want!"

CHAPTER VI.

RESULTS OF THIRTY YEARS OF AGITATION.

" The weapons of the whole world must leave me still unstained."—INSCRIBED ON THE HERO ROLAND'S HELMET.

THE improvement in the social or general condition of woman has been even greater than that recorded in the chapter on Legal and Legislative History. A few brief statistics will show the changes which thirty years have wrought.

Woman as Teacher.—Previous to 1840, women were employed only as teachers of summer schools, to "spell the men" during the haying season; and this only occasionally. They held no responsible position in any public school in the State. To-day from seven to eight women to one man are employed in all grades of this profession, and there are numerous instances where women are head teachers of departments, or principals of high, normal, and grammar schools.

Woman as Student and Professor.—Previous to 1825, girls could attend only the primary schools of Boston. In that year, through the influence of Rev. John Pierpont, the first high school for girls was opened in that city. There was a great outcry against this innovation ; and, because of the excitement in the community on the subject, and the *great number of girls* who applied for admission, the scheme was abandoned.

In the town of Plymouth, where the Pilgrim fathers and mothers first landed, when the question whether girls should receive any public instruction first came up in town meeting, there was great opposition to it. One gentleman objected, saying: "I am opposed to instructing girls. If we teach them—suppose I should be writing, a woman might come in and look over my shoulder and say, 'that word is spelled wrong,' and I should not like that! I am entirely opposed to instructing girls." The town, however, showed a more liberal spirit, and voted to give the girls one hour's instruction daily. This was in 1793.

In 1855, the Girls' High and Normal School

9

was established in Boston, and without let or hindrance has since continued in successful operation.

In 1867, the Lowell Institute and the Massachusetts Institute of Technology (both of Boston), advertised classes free to both sexes in French, mathematics, and in other advanced studies. Since that time Chauncy Hall School and Boston University have been opened to women, with the equal privileges of male students.

In 1878, the Girls' Latin School in Boston was founded. The establishment of this successful institution was the result of discussions on the subject of the education of girls, first brought before the public by Mrs. Emily Talbot and other ladies of Boston. High schools in almost all the towns and cities of the State have long been established, and in them the boys and girls of this good old Commonwealth are co-educated, and learn to become useful citizens—and voters.

Colleges for women have also been founded. Vassar, in Poughkeepsie, New York, (chartered in 1860), leads the list, and Wellesley and Smith have long been doing good university work. Thirty years ago, there was probably no college in the country, except Oberlin, to which women students were admitted. To-day 153 collegiate institutions in different parts of the United States invite their attendance.* Even conservative Harvard begins to melt a little under this regenerating influence, and invites women students through the doors of its "annex," to come and enjoy some of the privileges found within its sacred halls of learning. This was a late act of grace from a college whose inception was in the

---

* Oberlin was the first college in this country in which the co-education of the sexes was attempted. This institution was founded as a school in 1832, but soon afterwards it became an anti-slavery college, and admitted colored men and women as students. Those who did the most to place it on a secure foundation were Arthur Tappan, President Finney, Theodore D. Weld, Henry B. Stanton, and Rev. Charles Avery. In 1868, there were twenty-seven colleges in the United States, of which Oberlin was the noble pioneer. In 1881, in the discussion of General Burnside's "Educational Bill" in Congress, the fact was brought out that there are now one hundred and fifty-three colleges in the United States which admit women to their courses of study.

Among the women students who have done honor to Oberlin as *Alma Mater* may be mentioned the names of Lucy Stone, Antoinette Brown Blackwell, and Sally Holly.

mind of a woman longing for a better opportunity than the new colony could give to educate her afterwards ungrateful son.*

It might be explained here that the "Harvard
Annex," or "Private Collegiate Instruction for
Women," is not an organic part of the University itself. Under a certain arrangement, a limited number of women students are allowed a
few of the privileges of the men students of the
University. They are also permitted to use
some of the books belonging to the College
library, and attend a few of the College lectures.
No College building is appropriated for this
purpose, but recitation rooms are provided in
private houses. A witty Cambridge lady called
this mythical college the "Harvard Annex;" the
public adopted the name, and many people
suppose that there is such a hall or College
building. From the first annual report of the
"Private Collegiate Instruction for Women" it
appears that in 1879 twenty-seven women availed
themselves of the privilege of attending this course
of instruction.

* For Lucy Downing and Harvard College, see Appendix M.

These students go alone and unattended to the lectures and to the library of the College. A great change indeed, since the time when women first began to attend the Lowell Institute lectures! Then it was thought almost disgraceful for women to go to a public meeting without male protection, and they went with veiled faces, as if ashamed to be seen of men. It need not be written here how large a proportion of women go to make up the lecture and concert audiences of Massachusetts to-day; nor is it unusual that, either from choice or necessity, many of them go without male escort, and no one thinks the custom strange, or worthy of remark.

Miss Maria Mitchell was the first woman in the country to hold the position of college professor. She became Professor of Astronomy and Mathematics at Vassar, in 1866 Since that time women have become members of the faculty in several of the large colleges in the country. Professor Rachel Bodley, of Philadelphia, in a recent address, stated that the demand for women professors in schools and colleges exceeded the supply; and she urged upon the young women students of special sciences, to fit themselves for this position and for work in the laboratory.

Women as Physicians.—In the early days of the Commonwealth, women practiced midwifery, and were very successful. Anne Hutchinson, Mrs. Fuller and Sarah Alcock were the first women physicians in the State. Mrs. Janet Alexander, a Scotchwoman, was a well trained midwife. She lived in Boston and was always recognized as a good practitioner in her line by the leading doctors in that city.

Dr. John C. Warren, of Boston, invited this lady to come to this country. His biography, recently published, contains a short record of the matter in which he says: "We determined to recommend Mrs. Alexander. She was a Scotchwoman, regularly educated, and having Dr. Hamilton's diploma." Quite a storm was raised among the younger men physicians of Boston, by this attempted innovation, because they thought Dr. Warren was trying to deprive them of all profitable practice. But Mrs. Alexander, supported by Dr. Warren, and perhaps other physicians, continued successful practice, and educated her daughter in the same profession.

Nancy Clarke Binney was the first regular woman physician in Massachusetts.*

Dr. Harriot K. Hunt practised in Boston as early as 1835. She sought admission to the Harvard Medical School, and was many times refused. She was not what is called a "regular physician." In her day there existed no schools or colleges for the medical education of women, but she studied by herself, and acquired some knowledge of diseases peculiar to women. Her success was so great in her line of practice that she proved the need existing for physicians of her own sex.

Dr. Hunt's tussle with the medical faculty will long be remembered. She was the first woman in the State who dared assert her right to recognition in this profession. For this, and for her persistent efforts to secure for them a higher education, she deserves the gratitude of every woman who has since followed her footsteps into a profession over which the men had long held undisputed control.

*Dr. Elizabeth Blackwell was the first regular woman physician in America. She entered the Geneva Medical College, in New York, in 1847.

The first female medical college in New England was organized by Dr. Samuel Gregory, of Boston. This institution was chartered in 1856, under the name of the New England Female Medical College.* In 1868, it had graduated seventy-two women physicians, among whom were Dr. Lucy E. Sewall and Dr. Helen Morton, (who afterwards went to Paris, and studied obstetrics at Madame Aillot's Hospital of Maternity,) and Dr. Mercy B. Jackson. Dr. Jackson practised in Boston, and for five years before her death, filled the chair of Professor of Diseases of Children, at Boston University School of Medicine. She was a firm Suffragist, an able woman, and a good physician. She died December 13, 1877.

In 1859, the New England Female Medical College invited Dr. Marie E. Zakrzewska to the chair of Obstetrics, and at her suggestion, a hospital, or clinical department was added, in which students might receive practical education. Dr. Zakrzewska is a German by birth, and studied in

---

* The New England Female Medical College was, in 1874, by an act of the Legislature, united with Boston University School of Medicine.

the hospital *Charité* of Berlin. She came to America with a Prussian diploma of midwifery, but desiring further knowledge, went as student to the Western Reserve College, Hudson, Ohio, and graduated with a full diploma as Doctor of Medicine. She then went to New York, where, in conjunction with Dr. Elizabeth Blackwell she established the New York Infirmary for Indigent Women.

After three years service in the New England Female Medical College, Dr. Zakrzewska resigned her position, and in co-operation with Miss Lucy Goddard and Mrs. Ednah D. Cheney, established the New England Hospital for Women and Children. This institution was incorporated in 1863. Its avowed objects were · 1. To provide for women, medical aid of competent physicians of their own sex. 2. To assist educated women in the practical study of medicine. 3. To train nurses for the care of the sick.

The hospital opened in a dwelling house on Pleasant street, in Boston. It now occupies spacious buildings on Codman Avenue, Boston Highlands. The Maternity house is entirely separate from the main body of the hos ital. Its fifteen free beds have proved a beneficent charity to the poorer class of women. The sick and suffering are admitted to the privileges of the institution without distinction of color or nationality. Even error does not shut the poor woman from the comforts of the Maternity house. Its charity work, done through the free dispensary in Warrenton street, is also very great.

Its educational work is constantly on the increase. Six students are usually resident at the hospital, and several young women are kept in training as nurses for the sick.

In 1876, the New England Hospital had numbered among its students sixty-four women who were afterwards practising physicians. The Massachusetts names are Lucy E. Sewall, Helen Morton, C. Augusta Pope, Emily F. Pope, Emma L. Call, Adelaide A. Richardson, Julia Marchant, Seraph Frissel and Susan Dimock. From 1872 to 1875, the lamented Susan Dimock was resident physician at this "dear hospital," as she had called it in a written prayer found among her papers after her untimely death.*

Massachusetts has many other successful women physicians besides those who have graduated
from the New England Hospital for Women and
Children, who have been educated in the medical
schools in other states or countries. Among
these may be mentioned Dr. Lucy M. Hall,
resident physician at the Women's Prison at Sherborn — the only woman physician whose name
is found in the New England Medical Register,
for 1881.

Boston University is open to both sexes, with
equal studies, duties and privileges. This institution was incorporated in 1869, and includes
among other schools and colleges, a School of
Theology, a School of Law and a School of Medicine. William F. Warren, LL. D., is President
of the University, and the corporation is made up
of many distinguished men and women. Boston
University School of Medicine (Homœopathic),
was organized in 1873, I. Tisdale Talbot, M. D.,
Dean. Of the thirty-two lecturers and professors
who constitute the Faculty, five are women. These
are Mary J. Safford, M. D., Professor of Gynæ-
cology; Caroline E. Hastings, M. D., Professor

of Anatomy; Annie E. Fisher, M. D., and Martha J. Flanders, M. D., Lecturers on Diseases of Children; Adeline B. Church, M. D., Assistant Demonstrator in Clinical Medicine.

Since 1874, seventy-four women have graduated from this School, and of these, forty-two are now practising in Massachusetts. A fair average have attained to quite as extensive a practice as male physicians aspire to, and have also made for themselves a good reputation. It is the verdict of Dr. Talbot, that, as a rule, the women have fully equaled the men graduates in thoroughness of medical attainments. Besides those mentioned as belonging to the Faculty of Boston University School of Medicine, the following are among the best known names of women Homœopathic physicians now practising in Massachusetts: Arvilla B. Haynes, Laura M. Foster, Emily Metcalf, Mary A. Payne, Harriet H. Hodges, and Harriet J. Clisby.

Boston University School of Medicine and the Massachusetts Homœopathic College occupy extensive and elegant buildings on East Concord street, opposite the City Hospital. The School building contains three ample lecture rooms, including an amphitheatre capable of seating three hundred students; laboratories, a dissecting-room, museum, and an extensive medical library. The hospital contains forty beds devoted principally to acute diseases. During 1880, a large number of cases have been witnessed by the students, both men and women, and these and other hospital facilities have greatly increased the means of practical instruction. Of women in the dissecting-room it may be said, that they are quite as cool-headed and firm of nerve as are the men students. A Homœopathic Medical Dispensary has been established in connection with the Hospital, which has three separate branches in different parts of Boston. These are accessible to students, and from among the large number of patients who daily resort to them, there is excellent opportunity for the practical study of acute and chronic diseases. The medical colleges for men in many parts of the United States have long since been opened to women students, but "Fair Harvard," whose advantages in this direc tion are the greatest and most to be desired of any college in the country, has, up to this time, refused to admit women into its Medical School. The women students who still continue to apply to it for a medical education, have so far, been no more successful than was Harriot K. Hunt, who, nearly forty years ago (in 1847), knocked at its unyielding doors.

The Massachusetts Medical Society does not admit women doctors to membership, though the *regular* practitioners are generally willing to consult with them. They also seem ready enough to take advantage of their experience, and of the woman's insight into the diagnosis of special and peculiar cases. But so far as recognition by their brethren goes, the women physicians of the *regular school* in Massachusetts are no better off than they were in the beginning. The need of women in this profession had so long been felt by the community at large, that, whether *regular* or *irregular*, they have slowly and surely, and *in spite of the doctors*, made great headway in the profession. Where ten years ago, there was one woman physician, there are now scores, practising successfully in the different towns and cities in the State, and their names have become household words to the sick and suffering of their sex. Of woman's skill and success in this profession, there can be no longer any doubt. Even the doctors themselves do not venture to "disagree" on this point.

Woman in the Church.—Olympia Brown was the first settled woman pastor in the State. Her parish was at Weymouth Landing. In 1864 she petitioned to the Massachusetts Legislature "that marriages performed by a woman should be made legal." The Committee on the Judiciary, to whom the matter was referred, reported that no legislation was necessary as "marriages solemnized by women were already legal." Thus the Legislature of the State established the precedent, that "he" meant "she" under the law, in one instance at least. Phœbe M. Hanaford, Mary H. Graves and Lorenza Haynes were the first Massachusetts women to be ordained preachers of the Gospel. Rev. Miss Haynes has held prominent ministerial offices in Maine, where she is now settled; she has been chaplain of the Soldier's Home at Togus, and also chaplain of the Maine House of Representatives. Rev. Miss Brown was a noted speaker and worker during the late War of the Rebellion, and also during the Kansas struggle in 1867.

The Harvard Divinity School at Cambridge does not yet admit women students; but there are other theological schools in the State where a complete preparation for the ministerial profession can be obtained. There are now a score or two of women preachers in Massachusetts, and whether ordained after the manner of men preachers or not, they preach the word of God in sincerity and to good acceptance. Julia Ward Howe has often performed pulpit service during the last twelve years. Her pulpit is cosmopolitan; one of her most interesting preachings was to the blacks of St. Domingo. The women ministers of the State who bear the title of Reverend are Ellen G. Gustin, Mary H. Graves, Ada C. Bowles, Annie L. Shaw, and perhaps others.

The attitude of the Church towards the woman question has greatly changed within thirty years. There is now hardly any denomination, except the Catholic and the Episcopalian, which requires women to "keep silent in the churches," **or** refuses to let them take part in the deliberations of church or parish meetings. As early as 1869, women began to serve on committees, and to be ordained deaconesses of churches; and the Jews about that time first permitted women to take a certain part in the services of the synagogue.

Women also hold important offices connected with the different church organizations. They serve on the boards of state and national religious associations, and on boards of directors of church institutions. There are also missionary associations, both home and foreign, centenaries, Christian unions, and auxiliary associations, all officered and managed entirely by women. Even the treasurers of these large bodies are women, and their husbands or trustees are no longer required to give bonds for them.*

In 1880, the Massachusetts Woman Suffrage Association sent a memorial to the Monday

---

* In 1840, a woman could not legally be treasurer of even a sewing society without having some man responsible for her.

meetings of the Methodist, the Baptist, and the Unitarian ministers of Boston, in which they asked each one present to bring the question of suffrage for women in some way before his own congregation. No answer was received from the Baptist or the Unitarian ministers; but the Methodist ministers took the memorial up for discussion, Dr. Warren, president of Boston University, Rev. Dr. Cummings, and Rev. J. W. Bashford taking the affirmative. They reported the result substantially as follows: "We have carefully considered the subject, and we accord hearty and entire sympathy and co-operation favorable to the elevation of woman. . . . . For in Christ Jesus 'there is neither Jew nor Greek, there is neither bond nor free, there is neither male nor female.' They are all parts of one body. The place of woman in the church is every day becoming more important and conspicuous. . . . . To the women of the Suffrage Association we extend our sincere and cordial congratulations, and shall be pleased to afford them such aid in their good work as we may from time to time be able." At the late general conference of the Methodist Episcopal Church, the word "male" was stricken from the discipline, and the word "person" inserted in its place, in all cases save those that concerned the ordained clergy. Though there is this little "hitch" about ordaining women preachers, this denomination has indeed taken a long step in advance of its position in 1868, when Gilbert Haven entered the "procession." About that time, at a Monday meeting of Methodist ministers he made a speech in which he warned his brethren that, whether they wanted it or not, woman suffrage was sure to come "as soon as a few more of you old fogies are out of the way." *

Woman as Lawyer.—It is a notable fact, that in Massachusetts the "woman intruding element" has not as yet entered the so-called learned profession of the law. The State has had no Belva A. Lockwood, J. Ellen Foster, nor Myra Bradwell to plead for the legal rights of women before the Supreme Judicial Court. Only

* At the last Annual Meeting of the Massachusetts Woman Suffrage Association, held in January, 1881, six out of the twenty-four speakers were Methodist ministers.

one woman has yet dared to venture within the intricacies of the courts of law. This was Mary E. Stevens, the daughter and co-partner of Edward S. Stevens, conveyancer. Miss Stevens may have done a little outside law business, but she was not a member of the Bar, and therefore not a "regular" lawyer.

In Iowa, California, Illinois, Indiana, Michigan, Texas, Wisconsin, Minnesota Ohio, New York, and in the District of Columbia, women have been admitted to practice in the United States Courts, as well as in the courts of their respective states. Belva A. Lockwood and J. Ellen Foster are both admirable forensic lawyers.

It need hardly be said, that the Law School at Harvard is not open to women. Boston University, however, has long ago offered the advantages of its Law School to women students on the same terms on which men students are admitted. Women do not seem to avail themselves to any extent of this chance to study law. In its catalogue and circular for 1879–80 only one, Lelia Josephine Robinson, is found among its long lists of students. This young lady was born in Boston and is a direct descendant of Rev. John Robinson, the pastor of the Pilgrim Fathers. She entered Boston University School of Law in 1878, and has pursued her three years' course of study there in company with one hundred and fifty — more or less — men students. Miss Robinson graduated in the summer of 1881, and is the first woman lawyer who has ever graduated in Massachusetts. In March, 1881, she made her application for admission to the Bar, and Chief Justice Gray, desiring to hear an argument supporting her claims as a citizen, a hearing before the Court took place, April 23. She prepared, unaided, the brief from which Hon. Charles R. Train, her counsel, argued her case. In presenting her claim, Mr. Train admitted that it was a novel one : but in a very effective manner, he went on to state the cogent reasons why a woman who had carefully prepared herself for the profession of the Law, should be permitted to practice in the courts. At the close, Chief Justice Gray gave the opinion informally, that the laws, as they now exist, preclude woman from being attorney at law but he reserved the matter for the consideration of the full bench.   If the decision of the Supreme Judicial Court is adverse to Miss Robinson's claim, she will probably apply to the Legislature for a change of statute, so that "he" may mean "she" in the legal, as well as in the ministerial profession.   That body will probably follow the precedent established in 1875, and pass an act declaring that "no *person* shall be deemed ineligible to practice law by reason of sex!"   Miss Robinson gives a very pleasant testimony of the consideration, assistance and encouragement given her during her three years' course in the Law School, by professors, instructors and students.   Not a single word, act or look, has ever made her feel ill at ease, or out of place.   Boston University School of Law is the only law school in New England, or this side of Washington, D. C., that is open to both sexes.   No woman has yet graduated there, and three only have ever been there as students of law.   So far as known, there is only one woman lawyer in New England,— Miss Nash, of Portland, Maine.   It is to be hoped that Miss Robinson will persevere and gain legal entrance into her chosen profession, and that in

time, either she or some other "sweet girl gradu-
ate" will prove to the skeptical world with what
aptitude the female mind can deal with the "nice
sharp quillets of the law."

Woman in Art. The three best known women
sculptors in this country were born and bred in
Massachusetts. They are Harriet Hosmer, Margaret Foley and Anne Whitney. Harriet Hosmer
was the first to free herself from the traditions of
her sex and follow her profession as a sculptor.
When she desired to fit herself for her vocation
there was no art school east of the Mississippi
River where she could study anatomy, or find
suitable models. Margaret Foley, who, amid the
hum of the machinery in the Lowell cotton mills,
first conceived the idea of chiseling her thought
on the surface of a "smooth-lipped shell," was
obliged to go to Rome in order to get the necessary instruction in cameo cutting. There her
genius developed so much that she began to
model in clay and soon became a successful
sculptor in marble. Lucy Larcom, in her "Idyl
of Work," says of Miss Foley:

"That broad-browed delicate girl will carve at Rome,
                                                    "

A free art school in Boston was opened to women in 1867, and Anne Whitney was not obliged to go to Rome for instruction in the appliances of her art.   Harriet Hosmer and Margaret Foley have both made statues which adorn the public buildings and parks of their native country ; and Anne Whitney's statue of Samuel Adams which stands in Adams Square (formerly Dock Square), in Boston, speaks for itself, and is the crowning work of her genius.

No great work has yet been done by a Massachusetts woman in oil painting, but in water colors, and in decorative art, many women have excelled, first prizes in superiority of design having been taken by them over their men competitors. Lizzie B. Humphrey, Jessie Curtis, Mary Hallock Foote and Fidelia Bridges, take high rank as designers.   Helen M. Knowlton, a pupil of William M. Hunt, is a skillful artist in charcoal and has produced some fine pictures in this medium. Women form a large proportion of the students in the school of design recently opened in Boston.

A great deal of the ornamental painting now so fashionable on cards and all fancy articles is done by the deft fingers of women, and the woman artist, either amateur or artisan, is almost as common as the woman writer.

Of woman as actress and public singer, it would be unnecessary to speak, since she has the right of way in both these professions. Here, fortunately, the supply does not exceed the demand; consequently she has her full share of rights, and what is better, an equal amount of pay for her labor.

Woman as Journalist and Author.—In 1841, when Lydia Maria Child edited the *Anti-Slavery Standard*, Margaret Fuller the *Dial*, and Harriot F. Curtis and Harriet Farley the *Lowell Offering*, there were perhaps in New England (if in the country), no other well known women journalists or editors. Cornelia Walter of the *Evening Transcript* was the first woman journalist in Boston. To-day, women are editors and publishers of newspapers all over the United States; and the woman's column is a part of the make-up of many a leading newspaper. The names are almost numberless of women who furnish articles for the daily and weekly press, or are on the staff as correspondents or reporters. Sallie Joy White was the first regular woman reporter in Boston. She began on the *Boston Post*, a democratic newspaper, in 1870. Her first work was to report the proceedings of a woman suffrage meeting. She is now on the staff of the *Boston Daily Advertiser.* There are so many women who now write for the papers, one might almost say that the woman of brains who does not dabble in printer's ink is an exception.

Some of the best magazine writing of the time is done by women; one needs but to look over the table of contents of the leading periodicals to see how large a proportion of the articles are written by them. Really, the sex seems to have entered into and taken possession of what Carlyle called the "fourth estate,"—the literary profession, and they journey into unexplored regions of thought as well as into hitherto undiscovered countries to give the omnivorous modern reader something new to feed upon.

Among the Massachusetts women whose literary reputations are almost cosmopolitan, may be mentioned the names of Elizabeth Stuart Phelps, Harriet Prescott Spofford, Adeline D. T. Whitney, Caroline H. Dall, Louisa M. Alcott, Ednah D. Cheney, Elizabeth P. Peabody, Abby Morton Diaz, and Gail Hamilton.

One hundred years ago Massachusetts could boast of only two women poets; and one of them, Phillis Wheatley, was black and had been a slave. The women poets of the State have not increased in so large a ratio as have the writers of prose. In the verses of Julia Ward Howe, Helen Hunt Jackson, Elizabeth Stuart Phelps, Lucy Larcom, Anne Whitney, Sarah H. Palfrey and Annie T. Fields can be found the expression of the womanly element in the poetic thought of the State.

Woman as Speaker and Lecturer.—It has been mentioned what great opposition existed to women as public speakers when Abby Kelley Foster and Angelina Grimké appeared upon the anti-slavery platform. Even twenty years ago the number of women who dared to be heard before a small audience could be counted upon one's fingers. To-day, in Massachusetts alone,

Lucy Stone, Mary Ashton Livermore, Julia Ward Howe, Ednah Dow Cheney, Abba Goold Woolson, Mary F. Eastman, Kate Gannett Wells, Anna Garlin Spencer and a host of others are before the public, either as professional lecturers or speakers at clubs and private meetings.

Here, in particular, must be claimed the credit due the Woman's Rights movement. It cannot be denied that, but for the opportunity given them to speak upon its platform, many of the women now so celebrated as orators and lecturers would have remained mute and inglorious,—perhaps even forever unknown to an admiring public. The unpopular reform once needing so much the help of women speakers, became in time a helper to them. Upon the suffrage platform many a novice has first learned to think upon her feet, and to express her thoughts before a loving and appreciative audience; and from this humble beginning or stepping-place more than one woman lecturer in the State has mounted to a higher rostrum.

Woman as Office Holder.—The number of offices to which women are eligible, in this

State, has been enumerated in the chapter on Legal and Legislative History. As United States official, woman has not an extensive record. In 1862, Salmon P. Chase appointed the first woman postmaster. In 1881, of the 44,140 post offices in the United States, 4,000, or about one-tenth, are managed by women postmasters. Since the passage of the Act of Congress authorizing the appointment of married women to this office, their number has rapidly increased. The Postmaster General has always been favorable to women in the Department, and has appointed quite a number to clerkships which require that the incumbent shall have a superior education, and a knowledge of foreign languages. These superior women clerks in the Post Office Department at Washington now number in all between ninety and one hundred. Of woman's capacity as postmaster the opinion of the First Assistant Postmaster General is, that they "perform their duties with credit to themselves and honor to their country." Women postmasters are particularly popular in the small offices in the farming districts. In some rural sections the "post office" is a bureau or a table drawer in the

kitchen or fore-room, and it is much more con-
venient for a woman to have charge of its contents because she is always "at home" and
ready to receive and disburse the mail. There
are several women holding appointments at the
larger offices who have proved entirely competent
in the discharge of the duties incumbent upon
them, and (to quote again from headquarters),
they "are universally honest in money matters."

Through the efforts of the Association for the
Advancement of Women,* the Census Bureau

---

*The Association for the Advancement of Women, a
national organization, was projected in 1873 by "Sorosis,"
a woman's club in New York City. Its first congress was
held in that city in the Union League Theatre. Its first
president was Mary Ashton Livermore, and on the executive board were the names of representative women from
all parts of the United States. Since its formation it has
held an annual congress in New York, Illinois, Pennsylvania, Ohio, Rhode Island, Wisconsin, and lastly in Massachusetts. At these meetings a great variety of ethical subjects
are presented in papers or lectures written by women, and
they are freely discussed by the members present.

Since 1876, "A. A. W." has gradually drifted from the
control of its founders and Massachusetts women now
"turn the crank" of the machinery of the association.

Since the State has lost its former prestige of leadership
in national and political affairs, it may be that the women
of our ambitious Commonwealth are destined to take the
lead in discussing the ethical, social, and moral questions

has been opened to women. A committee of ladies from this association waited upon Gen. F. A. Walker, superintendent of the Census, and requested him to appoint a certain proportion of women as enumerators under the tenth Census Act of 1880. He responded favorably, and instructed the supervisors of the several districts to appoint women to this office when practicable. They were accordingly so appointed in many parts of the United States. Mr. Carroll D. Wright, supervisor of the district of Massachusetts was in favor of Gen. Walker's instructions, and out of the nine hundred and three enumerators appointed by him, thirty were women.* This was an exceedingly large proportion compared with the number appointed in states where supervisors were not in favor of women enumerators.

It may be well to add here, that organized bodies of women have latterly been recognized, and entertained officially, in Massachusetts as well as in other states. In 1880 Mayor Prince

---

* Mr. Carroll D. Wright's opinion of women enumerators is, that "on the whole they performed their work as well as the men."

of Boston received the Association for the Advancement of Women, and, in behalf of the city of Boston invited the members of that body to take an excursion to Deer Island. Here they were shown the reform school for boys and girls, one of the City institutions, and were provided with lunch at the expense of the city. Governor Long also received this Association at the State House, and in a graceful speech welcomed the members, coming as they did from all parts of the United States, to the hospitality of the Commonwealth.

Women are members and hold high positions in many of the state and national scientific and social science associations * They are officers as well as members of the Granges, and also of many other secret societies originally established for men alone. A National Society for Political Education, formed in 1880, invites

---

* The American Social Science Association was formed in 1865, and women were put on its board of officers. In 1865 the Boston Social Science Association was organized, and seven women were on its list of officers. These were the first large organizations in the country to admit women on an absolute equality with men.

women members, and has at least one woman on its board of officers. What would have been thought thirty years ago, if women had studied finance, political economy, banks and banking, money, currency, sociology and political science?

To show that in the march of events, the woman element is carried into all new enterprises, it will not be out of place here to make some mention of the Summer School of Philosophy at Concord, Massachusetts. This new school of Philosophy was founded in 1879. Its projectors were A. Bronson Alcott, Ralph Waldo Emerson, Professor W. T. Harris, Frank B. Sanborn, Professor Benjamin Pierce, Dr. H. K. Jones, Elizabeth P. Peabody and Ednah D. Cheney. On the list of lecturers for the summer of 1881, are the names of three women, Julia Ward Howe, Ednah D. Cheney and Elizabeth P. Peabody. Unlike the elder Schools of Philosophy, here the women students are in the majority, and they come from near and far, to spend a few weeks of their summer vacation in the enjoyment of this halcyon season of rest. Day after day they sit patiently on the æsthetic benches of the Hillside Chapel and bask "in the calm light of mild philosophy."

The Concord School is a school of Christian philosophy and morals, and its teachings are destined to be planted deep with roots far spreading in all the community of thought. Its seed was sown forty years ago, in what was called the Transcendental movement in New England. *That* could not become a permanent power, because it savored too much of Pantheism, and there was no executive force among its members. The Concord School finds in Mr. Sanborn its executive spirit, without which it could no more have come into existence at this time than its first seed could have been planted forty years ago without Mr. Emerson's and Mr. Alcott's ideal and conceptive thought.

Women in the Useful Occupations.—There has never been, from time immemorial, much difference of opinion concerning woman's right to do a good share in the drudgery of the labor of the world. But in the remunerative employments, before 1850, she was but sparsely represented. In 1840, when Harriet Martineau visited this country, she found to her surprise (in a free country) that there were only seven vocations, outside the home, into which the women of the United States had entered.* In contrast it is only necessary to mention that in Massachusetts alone, woman's ingenuity is now employed in over one hundred different branches of industry, many of which were once thought to be man's work alone. It cannot be added that for doing the same kind and amount of work women are paid men's wages.

Among the many rights woman has appropriated to herself must be included the "patent right." The charge has often been made that women never invent anything—but statistics on the subject declare that in 1880 patents for their own inventions were issued to seventy different women in the United States.†•

* These were, "teaching, needlework, keeping boarders, cotton mills, compositors, and folding and stitching in bookbindery." Following the New England mode of expression at the time, they may be classed differently, viz.: teachers, boarding-house keepers, help, (or servants), factory girls, compositors, workers in book bindery, tailoresses, milliners, mantuamakers, and dressmakers.

† Most of the inventions of women have to do with house-

According to the census of 1880, there are in Massachusetts 66,044 more women than men. In view of this fact it is fortunate that this great opening has been made, by which some at least of the "anxious and aimless" women of the State can earn an honest livelihood. To show what a large proportion of these surplus citizens of the Commonwealth are doing, it may be said, that in Boston alone, there are 20,000 shop and sewing girls, from 20,000 to 25,000 in domestic service, and 5,000 *lost* (or worse than lost) women.

The reform in public sentiment which made possible woman's great advance in the various departments of life, was not brought about without a vast deal of opposition on the part of certain public teachers and writers. Though the "rib" doctrine had long been ruled out of the pulpit, and the "hen" argument abandoned by

hold appliances. Among the past year's are a jar-lifter, a bag-holder, a pillow-sham-holder, dress-protector, two dust-pans, a washing-machine, a fluting-iron, a dress-chart, a fish-boner, a sleeve-adjuster, a lap-table, a sewing-machine-treadle, a wash-basin, an iron-heater, sad-irons, a garment-stiffener, a folding-chair, a wardrobe bed, a weather strip, a churn, an invalid's bed, a strainer, a milk-cooler, a sofa-bed, a dipper, a paper-dish, and a plating device.

the newspapers, prominent men were still found who were eager to speak and write against this new development of the race,—this feminine "birth of the time."

Dr. Bushnell's "Reform Against Nature," the first book of note written against woman's rights; Dr. Todd's "Dove in the Serpent's Nest"; Dr. Fulton's talk, both in and out of the pulpit, served to show the weakness of that side of the question. Later, Francis Parkman, Dr. J. G. Holland, Carlos White, and even some women writers, have added their so-called arguments, in the vain attempt to keep woman as they think "God made her." Such writings can be called nothing better than rubbish, since in them there is no logical reasoning against Woman Suffrage as a right. Indeed, to the arguments in favor of this reform, there has yet been no valid reply by anybody.

Much the stronger writers and speakers have been found on the right side of this question. The names of leading speakers have already been mentioned. Perhaps the most suggestive articles in favor were Mr. T. W. Higginson's

"Ought Women to Learn the Alphabet," published in the *Atlantic Monthly* of February, 1859, and Mr. Samuel Bowles's "The Woman Question and Sex in Politics," published at a later date in the Springfield *Republican*. "Warrington," in his letters to the same newspaper from 1868 to 1876, never failed to present a good and favorable argument on some phase of the woman question. Caroline Healey Dall's lectures before 1860, and her book "The College, the Market and the Court," published in 1868, were seed-grain sown in the field of this reform. Samuel E. Sewall's able digest of the laws relating to the legal condition of married women, and William I. Bowditch's admirable pamphlets, have done incalculable service.*

The newspaper itself, that great engine "who has her ambassadors in every quarter of the globe, her couriers upon every road," has slowly swung round, and is at last headed in the right direction. Quietly and surely the press has indoctrinated the people into a recognition of the importance of the Woman's Rights question.

* See note to page 116.

Reporters for the daily press in Massachusetts no longer write in a spirit of flippancy or contempt concerning the proceedings of Woman Suffrage meetings; and where is there an editor in the State of any account who would permit a member of the staff on his newspaper to report a woman's meeting in any other spirit than that of courtesy?

Public teachers occupying high position and presidents of colleges (not Harvard) have given pronounced opinions in favor of the reform. When such leading minds as those of Dr. Storrs, President Seelye and President Hopkins, proclaim it as their opinion that the time has come for women to take part in public affairs, it shows that both college and church are no longer in opposition to the advancement of women.

Said President Hopkins of Williams College, in 1875: "I would at this point correct my teaching in The Law of Love, to the effect that *home* is peculiarly the sphere of woman, and civil government that of man. I now regard the home as the joint sphere of man *and* woman, and the sphere of civil government more of an open question between the two."

Dr. Storrs, in 1879, in speaking of the position of women in the time to come, said: "It is in the midst of this movement that we stand, have been standing in these past years, and are to stand in the years to come. It cannot be arrested. The push of centuries is behind it. The strong instincts of human society are working for it, and with it, all the time. * * * No man can stop this, any more than he can set his foot against yonder tent pole, and say, '*I will arrest the revolution of the globe.*'"

The New England Women's Club, parent* of the modern women's clubs, and associations for the advancement of women, has been one of the greatest factors in the woman's rights movement. Though this club is not a suffrage (any more than it is a temperance, or a literary) club, its members have, in their work and in their lives, illustrated the doctrine of woman's equality with man.

---

* In 1836 there was a small woman's club of Lowell factory operatives, officered and managed entirely by women. This may be a remote first cause of the origin of the N. E. W. Club, since it bears the same relation to that flourishing institution, that the native crab does to the grafted tree.

The New England Women's Club was formed in February, 1868. A few ladies met at the house of Dr. Harriot K. Hunt, to consider a plan for organizing a club for women. Its avowed object was "to supply the daily increasing need of a great central resting place, for the comfort and convenience of those who may wish to unite with us, and ultimately become a centre for united and organized social thought and action."

Its first president was Caroline M. Severance. On the executive board were the names of Julia Ward Howe, Ednah D. Cheney, Lucy Goddard, Harriet M. Pitman, Jane Alexander, Abby W. May, and many others who have since become well known. This club held its first meetings in private houses, but it has for several years occupied spacious club rooms on Park street, in Boston. Julia Ward Howe is its president. The club has its own historian, and when this official gives the result of her researches to the public, there will be seen how many projects for the elevation of women and the improvement of social life, have had their inception in the brains of those who assemble in the parlors of the New England Women's Club.*

A thousand little streams have helped to swell the tide which has uplifted the sphere of woman's life. The modern novel has added its "winning wave." Its heroine is no longer an Amanda, a Malvina, or a Melissa, whose dove-like eyes are ever pleading for male protection. She is more often a female doctor, as in Charles Reade's novel, who saves the life of the hero, or, as in W. D. Howells' story, she is a brave New England girl, who travels from continent to continent, unprotected save by her own honor and her own pride.

The drama speaks too feebly on the right side of the woman question. No modern successful dramatist has made this "humour" of the times the subject of his play. An effort was made in 1879, by the executive committee of the New England Woman Suffrage Association, to secure

---

* In 1874, it projected the movement by which women were first elected on the School Committee of Boston, and also prepared the petition to be sent to the Massachusetts Legislature of 1879, the result of which was the passage of the law allowing women to vote for School Committees.

a woman suffrage play; but it was not successful, and there is yet to be written a counteractive to that popular burlesque, " The Spirit of '76 " It is to be regretted that the stage still continues to ridicule the woman's rights movement and its leaders; for, as Hamlet says:

> " The play 's the thing,
> Wherein I 'll catch the conscience of the king."

In summing up this brief history of the part taken by Massachusetts in the woman's rights movement, it would be needless to add that the cause is steadily advancing. Never, in the history of civilization, has woman held the political legal or social position that she does in Massachusetts to-day! New avenues of employment for her capacity are constantly being opened, and in every department of public trust to which she has been promoted, she has shown her ability. In this first hour of woman's triumph, it only remains for her to keep what she has gained, and use faithfully the new privileges which have come into her life.

Being a woman, or because she is a woman, is no longer any reason why she cannot do the thing for which she is best fitted. There should be **no** shrinking, from timidity or love of ease, when she is called upon to fill a public position, or to express her opinions by ballot at the polls. Home duties, ever sacred and nearest the true woman's heart, will be better and more wisely performed, if assisted by the knowledge and experience which contact with life and public affairs cannot fail to give. The fact is already patent that it is not so much "more life and fuller" that we want, for women, but that more women are needed for the wider life and the responsible positions waiting for them.

Trained leaders are needed — women strong of purpose, who are willing to confront the public as presiding officers, or as public speakers, and to guide wisely the large masses of their sex who have not yet learned to think for themselves. They have too long been led in flocks, like sheep; the time has come for better leadership.

More educated women doctors are needed; more lawyers, preachers, professors and teachers in the higher grades of schools and in laboratories. More women are called for who will be willing to sacrifice their time and their domestic ease and serve without compensation on School Committee boards. It is a noted fact that, especially in the towns of the State, there cannot be found enough educated women who are willing to have their names used as candidates for this office.

More plucky women who understand the law and know how to use the newly-acquired "inalienable right of all American citizens," are needed to go to the assessor's office, to the caucus, and to the polls. More women are needed in the "fourth estate,"— not only as novelists, story-tellers, or journalists, but also as writers on ethical, moral and social questions, as dramatists, and as the biographers of their own sex. Historians are needed, who shall give the record of nations and events from the woman's standpoint, and include in the story of a people that which is often ignored,—the part taken by their sex in the occurrences of the times. Historians also are needed who will expose to public execration the woman side in the horrors of war, and who will give to future generations a fairer estimate of the character of the sex of which God has made one-half the human race, than has come down to us through the Hindoo, the Greek, the Roman, and sometimes the Christian literature.

To sum up the progress of the woman movement in all parts of the civilized world, it is well to begin with the record of its advance in our own country. Massachusetts is by no means ahead in the march of this great reform. Other states in the Union have more than kept pace with her, and many of them have made laws to improve the legal and social condition of woman. School Suffrage laws have been enacted in New Hampshire, Vermont,* Connecticut, New York, Colorado, Nebraska, Minnesota, Oregon, Kansas, Michigan and Arizona Territory.

Constitutional amendments giving women the right of suffrage, have just been passed by the Legislatures of Oregon, Nebraska and Indiana.

---

* By a law passed Dec. 18th, 1880, the women of Vermont are eligible for the office of superintendent of schools, and of town or city clerk. In March, 1881, Miss Electa F. Smith was chosen city clerk in Vergennes, Vermont, and a great many of the towns elected women for school superintendents.

These proposed amendments cannot become a part of the constitution until they are submitted to the men voters of the State for their ratification. In Nebraska the Suffragists are very active, and in order to enlighten the men who will be called upon to vote upon the matter in 1883, they have started a. *Western Woman's Journal,* whose motto is, "An aristocracy of sex is repugnant to a republic."* From a statement in the columns of this paper, it appears that seventy-four out of the eighty-eight established newspapers in Nebraska are in favor of the proposed amendment

In Indiana, a bill securing presidential suffrage to women came within a few votes of passing the House of Representatives. In the same progressive and wide-awake State women hold many prominent positions. Mrs. Emma A. Winsom has just been elected State librarian. In Iowa a woman has held this office since 1870. The present incumbent is Mrs. S. B. Maxwell. In other states where the suffrage question is not

---

* Hon. Erasmus M. Correll, the editor of this paper, was a member of the Nebraska Legislature, and the leader of the House in advocating the Woman Suffrage Amendment.

so largely agitated, women hold State offices. In the Legislature of Nevada Miss Kittrell is copying clerk, and like a man, she took the oath of allegiance to support the constitution, and not bear arms against the State. In Tennessee, Mary Grizzard is clerk of the State House of Representatives.

Maine and Minnesota have each made efforts to amend their constitutions, so that the women can exercise the full right of suffrage. California and Pennsylvania are asking for presidential suffrage. Rhode Island, always active in the good cause, is working for school suffrage. Michigan and Iowa are working steadily for woman's rights as a citizen of their own go-ahead states. In the Wisconsin Legislature, a Woman Suffrage amendment to the State constitution was, by a very close vote, recently defeated. Missouri has just begun to deliberate on the Woman Suffrage question. Bright little Kansas, a State rooted in principle and always on the right side, is asking for full suffrage for its women citizens. In this State husband and wife have the same property rights, and the same rights in their children. There the women teachers receive the same pay as the men for equal service. Illinois allows its women to vote in municipal elections. The women of New Jersey are struggling to regain their lost right of suffrage. A bill to prohibit the disfranchisement of the women of the state, was defeated in the New York Assembly in May, 1881, by just six votes. If this bill had passed, the women of New York would have become voters on the same terms with men at all elections.

In Wyoming Territory women have enjoyed all the political rights, privileges and responsibilities of men for the past eleven years, and they vote as regularly at the elections. The verdict of the leading newspaper in the State, on woman's voting, is this: " Not a solitary instance has ever occurred in which the exercise of their rights has been productive of any evil results. * * There can't be found a man in Wyoming to-day who is opposed to, or dissatisfied with the result of Woman Suffrage." In Utah Territory women vote under certain conditions. In far distant Omaha, the voices of the women send this message to their representatives: "Tell the members of the Legislature that we want to vote." When the Constitution of Texas was revised, in 1876 the word "male," either by accident or design, was left out and the women of that state have the right to vote on all questions relating to municipal or state government.

Even the American Indian, as early as 1870, began to scent the trail of the woman's rights movement, and in one tribe—the Otoe—many of the squaws refused to do all the work, declaring that they would not cook for the men unless they helped them do some of the work around the wigwams. In 1880, Bright Eyes, an Indian maiden, was sent to Washington by one of the most powerful tribes on the continent—the Poncas—to represent to the Government the rights and the wrongs of her people. Does not the world move?

The echoes of the 1850 convention, held in Massachusetts and in Ohio, travelled across the ocean, and the answer came back from England. Woman Suffrage or Woman's Rights under the law had never been heard of there until that time, though the ruler of the kingdom was a woman. To-day, the suffragists of England are busy, and large meetings are frequently held in the interest of the cause. At Bristol, in 1880, over 3000 women assembled to hear arguments presented, and devise means to further the reform. A memorial was prepared which stated that there were over 500,000 rate payers in the United Kingdom, who were deprived of the power of voting in the election for Members of Parliament because they were women, and they prayed "that a measure might be introduced by her Majesty's ministers to extend parliamentary franchise to women rate payers and land owners in boroughs and counties."

A great Suffrage meeting was held in Birmingham in February, 1881, which was attended by over 4,000 persons. A woman presided, and women speakers alone addressed the vast audience. The chief subject of discussion was the recognition by government of woman's claims to the parliamentary franchise. In England, women rate payers have the right to vote in all local elections of poor-law guardians, church-wardens, overseers, auditors and other local officials.   In 1881, ten women were elected poor-law guardians. Among them were the Dowager Marchioness of Lothian and Miss Florence Davenport Hill.

On the London school board, nine women serve as members and two as salaried officers; and by a vote of the Board, in 1881, women are eligible to the office of school inspector.   In many parts of England, property-holding women can vote under certain restrictions.   The Married Woman's Property Bill, presented to Parliament in March 1881, provides for a thorough change in the condition of the women of England as regards property rights.   Under its provisions woman is treated as a reasonable being, and not as an infant incapable of making a bargain, or fulfilling a contract save through her husband's sanction. When this bill becomes a law, the legal subjection of English women will be at an end, so far as money matters go.

The *London Athenæum*, in a recent number, stated that a memorial was being prepared by an influential committee of the non-resident members of the Senate of the Cambridge University, in favor of granting the degree of A. B. to women. Among the signers were Earl Spencer, Canon Barry and J. E. Gorst, M. P. What will the American Cambridge University (known as Harvard) say, if this great conservative English College gets the start of it, and is the first to confer upon woman the degree of Bachelor of Arts?

Since the first chapters of this book went to press, the great news has come from England that Cambridge University has opened her gates, broadly, freely and without barriers of any kind, to all women who desire to become co-students with men. In March 1881, the senate of Cambridge University by a large vote (398 to 32) decided to admit women students of Girton and Newnham to be formally examined and classified among the candidates for honors. Residence is allowed to such students in two of the college buildings, or within the precincts of the University. This is a great event in the history of the struggle for equal educational privileges for women and men.

Scotland is active in the Woman Suffrage

movement. It has a National Society, and its annual meeting held recently at Edinburgh was presided over by Mrs. Duncan M'Laren.

In the Isle of Man a bill with certain property qualifications, giving Suffrage to women, passed the House of Keys; and January 5, 1881, Queen Victoria in council gave her royal assent, thus establishing the principle of Woman Suffrage in parliamentary government within the British Islands. The act at once came into force and was formally promulgated on Tynwald Hill,* Isle of Man. The House of Commons is more than likely to follow the good example of the House of Keys, since the Queen has declared her recognition of the rights of her women subjects.†

The echoes of the American Conventions travelled far beyond the mother country, and have since reverberated from all parts of the civilized world. In France the Suffrage Move-

---

* "Once on the top of Tynwald's formal mound
    (Still marked with green turf circles narrowing
    Stage above stage) would sit this Island's King,
    The laws to promulgate, enrobed and crowned."
                                        WORDSWORTH.

† See Appendix N.

ment is steadily advancing, and the cry of "Liberty, Equality and Fraternity" begins to have a real meaning to the women citizens of that fair country. The first International, Woman's Rights Congress was held in Paris, in August, 1878, during the Great Exposition. It lasted more than two weeks, and closed with an elegant banquet, in which distinguished men and women from all parts of the world participated. There were two Presidents of the Congress: M. Henri Martin, and Julia Ward Howe,—"Meeses Ouardow," as the French president called that lady when he introduced her to the vast audience. Delegates to this Congress were present from many different countries, and several Italian ladies took active part in the deliberations. America was represented by Julia Ward Howe, T. Wentworth Higginson, Theodore Stanton, (son of Elizabeth Cady Stanton), and perhaps others.

The subjects discussed at the different sessions were:

1st. Historical, or woman's condition as presented by history.

2d. Educational, and all hygienic questions touching women and children.

3d. Woman's Work and Wages.

4th. Woman's Position before the Law.

In the 16th century, when Françoise De Saintonges made an attempt to found schools for the girls of France, she was hooted in the streets; and her father thought she must be possessed of demons, to think of such a thing as educating women. To-day, France has established intermediate schools, and Henri Martin, the historian, is projecting a series of colleges all over the country, for the higher education of French girls.

The Sorbonne long ago opened its lecture rooms to classes composed entirely of young girls under twenty years of age. The Sorbonne, or university of Paris, is the greatest literary institution in France. As early as 1878, it conferred the degree of A. B. upon women students. A French lady, Hubertine Auclert, an advocate of woman suffrage, lately refused to pay taxes, urging that as women are not allowed to vote, it was unjust that they should be taxed. Her furniture was seized, and the majesty of the law was sustained against her vain protests. Her story is admirably told in Alexander Dumas' "Les Femmes qui Tuent, et Les Femmes qui Votent." (The Women who Kill, and The Women who Vote.) M. Dumas strongly favors suffrage for the women of France. He says: "At first it will make a sensation, then it will become fashionable, after that a habit, then an experience, then a duty, and at last a blessing."

In February 1881, a great Convention was held at the Sala Dante in Rome, to agitate the question of Universal Suffrage. At this convention the claims of women were earnestly presented. Two women only — Elena Burelli and Signora Anna Maria Mozzoni — had seats as delegates. After some opposition on the part of the convention, resolutions were passed asserting the right of all Italian men and women to become voters. The passage of the resolution in which women were included, was due in great part to the persistent eloquence of Signora Mozzoni.

In Sweden, the old university town of Upsala, in 1859, granted the right of Suffrage to fifty women owning real estate, and to thirty-one doing business on their own account. This was secured through the influence of Frederika Bremer, who was not ashamed to shed happy tears when the news reached her. Through her influence, women students had already been admitted to the Musical Academy and the Academy of Fine Arts, at Stockholm.*

In St. Petersburg, Russia, at the first election for a municipal council, in 1881, all property-owning women were allowed to vote.

Spain, almost the last country from which one might expect to hear good news on the woman question, has just admitted women to lectures and degrees in her colleges. This was accomplished in spite of vigorous opposition on the part of members of the Superior Council of Education. Many women students won prizes and honors during 1880 in some of the Spanish universities.

Municipal suffrage is exercised by the women of Cape Colony, in Africa. New Zealand and Australia, have each made efforts to secure political rights and a higher education for women.

* See "The College, the Market and the Court." By Caroline H. Dall. Boston, Lee and Shepard.

In India an attempt has been made to abolish the Zenana system, and in both these countries the women themselves are struggling to be released from their degrading condition of servitude. Round the world from far Bombay comes a letter, in March, 1881, in which the writer says: "Bombay allows its women to vote on the same terms with its men, in the regulation and control of its municipal affairs." As early as 1870, said Lydia Maria Child, the suffrage movement was felt in Asia, some action being taken there to free the women from the iron rule of their Mussulman husbands. From far-away Japan, not long ago came the news that widow Kusanoe Kita had refused to pay her taxes, because she considered it "an injustice to be required to pay equal taxes with other heads of families when equal rights were not granted."

Even in the harems of Turkey the women are beginning to assemble to listen to speakers from another country, who have brought to them a doctrine not found in the religion of Mahomet,— the doctrine that they have souls, the same as their masters, and that the time has come for their deliverance from moral and intellectual slavery.

The most hopeful sign of the continued success of this great reform, is found in the fact that the women themselves, of all nations, are getting ready to work for their own emancipation from the bondage of centuries. The women are "up in America, and they are already past their first sleep in Persia." For them the hour has indeed struck, the morning light has dawned, and they are forever awakened to freedom and to independence.

APPENDIX.

A.

"OBSERVATIONS ON THE RIGHTS OF WOMEN."

BY HANNAH MATHER CROCKER. 1818.

THIS little book is worthy of mention, from the fact that it is probably the first publication of its kind in Massachusetts, if not in America. The whole title of the book is, "Observations on the Rights of Women, with their appropriate duties agreeable to Scripture, reason and common sense." Mrs. Crocker, in her introduction, says—"The wise author of Nature has endowed the female mind with equal powers and faculties, and given them the same right of judging and acting for themselves as he gave the male sex." She further argues that, "According to Scripture, woman was the first to transgress and thus forfeited her original right of equality, and for a time was under the yoke of bondage, till the birth of our blessed Saviour, when she was restored to her equality with man."

This is a very fine beginning, and would seem to savor strongly of the modern woman's rights doctrine; but, unfortunately, the author, with charming inconsistency, goes on to say,—"We shall strictly adhere to the principle of the impropriety of females ever trespassing on masculine grounds: as it is morally incorrect, and physically improper." In the book itself, the author cites with admiration many illustrious women who have "trespassed on masculine ground." Among them are Zenobia, Jane of Flanders, Elizabeth of England, and Oberach, queen of

Otaheite. The last named carried a sea captain (according to his own account) "over a marsh with as much ease as he could a little child." In speaking of Mary Wollstonecraft, Mrs. Crocker says, that while that celebrated woman had a very independent mind, and her "Rights of Woman" is replete with fine sentiments, yet, she continues, patronizingly, "we do not coincide with her respecting the total independence of the sex." Mrs. Crocker evidently wanted her sex to be not too independent, but just independent enough.

B.

THE WORLD'S ANTI-SLAVERY CONVENTION.

WHEN the American Anti-Slavery Society was formed, in 1833, some of the women present at the meeting made speeches, and the convention passed a vote of thanks to women for their zeal and interest in the cause. This society always encouraged women to speak against slavery, and it did not disapprove of their serving as officers of town or county societies.

In 1835, the society wished to delegate Mrs. Lydia Maria Child to visit England in the interests of the Anti-Slavery cause, and in 1837 it endeavored to secure her services as travelling lecture agent. The same year it offered the Misses Grimké a commission to enter the field as lecturers upon the evils of slavery. Previous to 1838, Abby Kelley had been speaking on the platform of women's Anti-Slavery meetings, but in that year as agent of the American Anti-Slavery Society, she came before public audiences composed of both men and women.

At the sixth annual meeting of the American Anti-Slavery Society, in May, 1839, an attempt was made for the first time to exclude women from active membership.

A motion was made by a clergyman that none but men should have their names placed upon the roll; but this motion was rejected by an overwhelming majority. The same year it chanced * that a woman was put on a committee to "examine and report" on the publication of the annual report. This caused a great commotion among the men members; but there was no open revolt until 1840, when, for the first time, a woman was elected on the business committee of the society. In consequence of this action, a minority of the members withdrew and formed another anti-slavery society. This division afterwards extended through many of the State and local Anti-Slavery organizations.

The World's Anti-Slavery Convention was first projected by the English abolitionists. When the American Anti-Slavery Society was invited to send delegates, it responded by adopting the following resolutions, offered by David Lee Child, at its annual meeting held in New York, May 12th, 1840:

"*Resolved:* That the American Anti-Slavery Society regards with heartfelt interest the design of the ' World's Convention' about to assemble in London, and anticipates from its labors a powerful and blessed influence upon the condition and prospects of the victims of Slavery and prejudice, wherever they are found.

"*Resolved:* That our beloved friends, William Lloyd Garrison, Nathaniel Peabody Rogers, Charles Lenox Remond, and Lucretia Mott, be and they hereby are appointed delegates, to represent this Society in the said Convention, and we heartily commend them to the confidence and love of the universal abolition fraternity.

"*Resolved:* That the Anti-Slavery enterprise is the cause of universal humanity, and as such, legitimately calls together the WORLD'S CONVENTION,— and that this Society

* "It chanced (Almighty God that chance did guide)."
[Spenser's Faerie Queene.]

trusts that that Convention will fully and practically recognize, in its organization and movements, the EQUAL BROTHERHOOD of the entire HUMAN FAMILY, without distinction of color, sex, or clime."

The delegates from other anti-slavery societies in the United States, were George Bradburn, Wendell Phillips, Ann Greene Phillips, Henry B. Stanton, Elizabeth Cady Stanton, Professor William Adams, Rev. Henry Colver, Rev. Nathaniel Greene, Rev. Eben Galusha, James Mott, James G. Birney, C. Edwards Lester, Sarah Pugh, Mary Grew, Elizabeth T. Neale, (now Mrs. Sidney Howard Gay), Emily Winslow Taylor, Col. J. P. Miller, Isaac Winslow, Abby Kimber, Abby Southwick, Rev. Henry Grew, and perhaps others.

Seven of these delegates had arrived early, and on finding that the women of their number were not to be admitted to their seats in the Convention, they framed a protest against such exclusion. These were Professor William Adams, James Mott, C. E. Lester, Isaac Winslow, Wendell Phillips, Jonathan P. Miller, and George Bradburn. Mr. Garrison, in his report read at the annual meeting of the Massachusetts Anti-Slavery Society, in January, 1841, gave a brief account of this "conference," as he called it; for, true to his principles on the question of the equality of human rights, he would not call a meeting in which women had no recognized part, a "World's Convention." He said:

" Though such a Convention was called, no such Convention was held. The Committee of the British and Foreign Anti-Slavery Society declared the meeting to be a mere 'Conference' with themselves, and in fact prescribed its rules and regulations, etc., etc. * * * The American, Massachusetts and Pennsylvania Societies chose as their representatives, among others, certain women of great moral worth, intelligence and philanthropy; but these were scornfully shut out from the Convention on account of their sex! * * * Their right was eloquently sustained by Wendell Phillips, Prof. Adams, George Bradburn, Dr. Bowring, Col. Miller, Mr. Ashurst, and others. * * *

"Messrs. Garrison, Rogers, Remond and Adams, delegates to the convention, did not arrive in season to participate in the discussion. On ascertaining, however, what that body had done, they very properly refused to become members of it, and accordingly took their seats in the gallery."

Dr. John Bowring and William H. Ashurst were English abolitionists. Some of the English abolitionists did not take Mr. Garrison's view of the equality of human rights, and one of them gave to the world his private opinion of this "woman intruding delusion," of which the following is an extract:

CAPTAIN CHARLES STUART'S PRIVATE CIRCULAR.

"In December, 1833, an Anti-Slavery Society was formed in the United States of North America. The demand for it was extreme, for the Slave system of the United States was the most desperately corrupt and ferocious which existed. The principles and objects of the Anti-Slavery Society thus formed were eminently excellent, and the means which it adopted for the attainment of its glorious object were perfectly in keeping, for the *first four years,* with its noble principles.

"But, in the course of 1837, *new* opinions began to be broached, and one of these gradually assumed the position that 'whatever is morally right for a *man* to do, is morally right for a *woman* to do,' and, therefore, women ought to be intruded as delegates, debaters and managers, into mixed societies of men and women. This insane innovation, at first, had so dubious a form, that its real character scarcely appeared; but as soon as this became evident, it was vigorously resisted. Resistance, however, only aggravated the zeal of its advocates, and the *new truth*, as they call it, quickly assumed such importance in their eyes and was so offensively intruded by them into all the proceedings of the Society, that *they* who conscientiously resisted it had no alternative but to submit to it or to separate themselves. I was one of the many who preferred the latter alternative without hesitation. The separation took place early in 1840; that of the leading Society in New York in May, 1840. At the division on the question, the Innovators were found the most numerous, and of course, the original name of ‘The *American* Anti-Slavery Society’ remained with them. But they who rejected the innovation, having fewer votes present, took a new name,—‘The *American* and *Foreign* Anti-Slavery Society.’

    *   *   *   *   *   *   *

“ Under these circumstances, the *American*—or *woman-intruding* — Anti-Slavery Society sends Agents to this country, Messrs COLLINS and REMOND, to beg our money. But let us remember that, whatever countenance we give to these gentlemen, or this agency, will go more directly to strengthen a pernicious party in the United States than to aid the general cause of Abolition. The errors of the advocates of justice are often more ruinous to righteousness than all the hostility of open enemies. By such aid Britain would be identified, as far as it goes, with the rhapsodists of the United States; and the sacred and powerful influence exercised so nobly and so beneficially by the late London Convention, in decidedly and at once rejecting the woman-intruding delusion, would be paralyzed or lost,—liberty would be wounded anew by the blunders of her friends,—while they who love her more sanely, and who plead her cause unentangled with the snare, would be enfeebled by the encouragement given to the dogmatism and delusions of their adversaries.”

The “ rhapsodists of the United States,” came after this

to be called Garrisonians. The issue between the Foreign and the American Anti-Slavery Society was substantially the same as that between the Garrisonians and the anti-Garrisonians,—it was the "woman-intruding element." In the beginning it was like a cloud, no bigger than a man's hand; but it soon began to grow, and in a few years it had spread so that even the most short-sighted of weather prophets could see that a great change was about to take place in the political and social atmosphere of the time.

C.

THE LOWELL OFFERING AND ITS WRITERS.

THE *Lowell Offering* was first published in 1840, by Abel C. Thomas, pastor of a Universalist Church in Lowell Massachusetts. In the second number of the magazine is an account of a social meeting of the young people of his parish, called the Improvement Circle. The members of this Circle, most of them operatives in the Lowell mills, were required to furnish original contributions to be read at the meetings. These were in prose and in verse, and were so well written and accumulated so fast, that Mr. Thomas, into whose hands they were entrusted, conceived the idea of publishing them. To this gentleman must be given the credit of bringing before the public these productions; and too much honor cannot be awarded to him for believing in the capabilities of the young people under his charge, and for utilizing the talent which he found. Mr. Thomas, who has recently died, little thought, perhaps, what would be the result of his efforts to encourage the young people of his church and community to express their thoughts on paper. But for his Improvement Circle, the *Lowell Offering* might never have been heard of, and its writers, if this impetus had not been given to their **talents,** would never have thought themselves capable of any success in this direction.   To improve and cultivate the mind was the great injunction urged by this good man, upon **the** young men and women of his time.

Mr. Thomas conducted the *Offering* for two years.   Then he left Lowell for another parish, and it passed into the hands of Miss Harriet Farley and Miss Harriot F. Curtis, both operatives in the Lowell mills.   Under their joint editorship the magazine, which never paid expenses, lasted till 1849, when it was discontinued, for want of means, and perhaps "new contributors."   The *Offering* was a small, thin magazine, with one column to the page.   On the outside cover, in 1845, it had for a vignette a young girl, simply dressed, with feet visible and sleeves rolled up.   She had a book in one hand and her shawl and bonnet were thrown over her arm.   She was represented as standing in a very sentimental attitude, contemplating a bee-hive on her right hand.   In the background, as if to shut them from her thoughts, was a row of factories.   The motto was :

"The worm on the earth
May look up to the star."

This was rather an abject motto and one not suited to the independent spirit of most of the contributors.   A better one was soon adopted, from Gray—the verse beginning :

"Full many a gem of purest ray serene."

It finally died under the motto :

"Is Saul also among the prophets?"

When Dickens visited this country, in 1842, he went into the Lowell factories, and a copy of the *Offering* was presented to him.   He speaks of it as follows :

"They have got up among themselves a periodical, called the *Lowell Offering*, whereof I brought away from Lowell four hundred good solid pages, which I have read from beginning to end. Of the merits of the *Lowell Offering*, as a literary production, I will only observe—putting out of sight the fact of the articles having been written by these girls after the arduous hours of the day—that it will compare advantageously with a great many English annuals." Selections from the *Offering* were printed in England, under the auspices of Harriet Martineau, who was very much interested in the publication. The volume was called "Mind among the Spindles."

The magazine was favorably received by the press generally. Even the *North American Review*, whose literary *dictum* was more autocratic than it is to-day, expressed a fair opinion of its literary merit. It said :—

"Many of the articles are such as to satisfy the reader at once, that if he has only taken up the *Offering* as a phenomenon, and not as what may bear criticism and reward perusal, he has but to own his error, and dismiss his condescension as soon as may be." This good opinion of the literary merits of the articles was, perhaps, due to the fact, that at this era of American magazine literature, what a writer had to say was of much more importance to the critic than the position of the predicate in his sentences, or the peculiar style of English in which they might happen to be written. The fact was often disputed that a "factory girl" could write for or edit a magazine,—since she had hitherto been considered little better than the loom or frame she tended. Enquiries on the subject came to the editors from different parts of the country, and questions like the following were often put to them : "Do the factory girls really *write* the articles published in the *Offering?*" or, "Do you print them just as they are sent ?" or "Do you revise or re-write them?" In the preface to the first volume, the editor answered these questions. He says:—"The articles are all written by factory girls, and *we do not* revise or re-write them. We have taken less liberty with them than editors usually take — with other than the most experienced writers." In spite of this assertion the charge continued to be made, that it could not be possible that females occupied in labor so low as factory life could be capable of such a literary undertaking. One gentleman went so far as to offer to give one of the editors (Miss Farley) twelve dollars, if she could point out to the public twelve original articles in the three last issues of the magazine. She pointed out twelve such articles in *one* of the numbers so designated.

As an excuse for any of the literary demerits of the magazine, the editor said to the critics,—"In estimating the talent of the writers of the *Offering*, the fact should be remembered that they are actively employed in the mills for more than twelve hours a day; and critics must be sensible that a day of constant manual labor though not excessive, must in some measure unfit the individual for full mental development. The productions in this volume will show how much of thought and aspiration is to be found among a class of people of whom little has been known." William Schouler of the *Lowell Journal* published the *Offering* in 1845, and his young sub-editor William S. Robinson wrote favorable notices of the magazine, and when he could do so, without letting "the editor step aside to make way for the friend," sometimes admitted its writers into the columns of that leading Whig newspaper. It may be added here, that this gentleman, in his zeal for the writers of the *Lowell Offering* went so far as to take one of the least known among them as his companion for life.

The contributions to the *Offering* were upon a great variety of subjects. Allegories, conversations on Physiology, Astronomy, and other scientific subjects; dissertations on poetry; the beauties of nature, flowers, etc.; didactic pieces on highly moral and "pious" subjects; translations from French and Latin; poems; stories of factory and other life; sketches of local New England history,—and sometimes the chapters of a novel, ran through its pages. The criticism was often made, that the operatives wrote too much on the "Beauties of Nature." To this, one of

the contributors "Ella" (probably Harriet Farley) answered, and gave as excuse :—"We are so long and constantly shut out from the sweet voices of the natural world;
yet its influences are still upon our captive souls, like the
impress of an engraver upon the rocks which support a
ruined fountain. The moss of years, and the lichens fed
by an impure atmosphere, may veil the tracery; but it is
still there, and has given its impress to the outward con-
formation of the over-spreading mould." The author
might have said with Emerson, if his "World-soul" had
then been printed,

> "And be sure the all-loving Nature
> Will smile in a factory."

The same author (in 1840) wrote an article on "Woman's
Rights," in which were so many familiar arguments in favor
of the equality of the sexes, that it might have been the
production of the pen of Lucy Stone or Elizabeth Cady
Stanton, but for this difference, that, though the writer felt
sure of her ground, she was too timid to maintain it against
the world,—and towards the end throws out the query,
"whether public life is, after all, woman's most appropriate and congenial sphere?" It is a curious coincidence,
that at this date the Anti-Slavery party, the great party of
freedom and equality, was at the point of division on this
very question.

There is a certain flavor in all the *Lowell Offering* writings, both in prose and verse, which reminds one of the
books read by the authors and the models they followed in
their compositions. The poetry savors of Mrs. Sigourney,
Mrs. Hemans, Miss Landon, Mrs. Barbauld, Milton, Pope,
Cowper, and Hannah More. Byron's sardonic vein is
copied by one or two of the most independent minds
among them. It must be remembered that this was before
the age of American poetry, and that the laurels of Longfellow, Lowell, Whittier, and Holmes had yet only budded.
When the poems of Longfellow and Whittier came out,

they were a new revelation to the girl of the factory period. The book as soon as received was lent from one to another all over the neighborhood, and the eager reader staid all day in her room on Sunday, or sat up all night to read the coveted volume. Many of them learned favorite poems, and repeated them to others less fortunate in being able to borrow the book. Some of these, now pretty old girls, still repeat to their children the well-remembered lines.

The prose models of writing were "The Spectator," "Miss Sedgwick's Letters," "The Vicar of Wakefield," "The Lady of the Manor," Lydia Maria Child's writings, "Stephens's Travels in Yucatan, Mexico, etc.," and Sunday-School books. Novels and dramatic writings were tabooed, by the puritanical spirit which controlled the daily walk of the average New England girl; even Walter Scott and Shakespeare were under the ban of the evangelical churches at this time. But the more free-thinking of them, who had wandered a little from the fold, towards the Unitarian or Universalist churches, took from the circulating library and read with delight such novels as "Evelina," "Alonzo and Melissa," "The Three Spaniards," "Charlotte Temple," "Eliza Wharton," "Maria Monk," "The Children of the Abbey," "The Arabian Nights," and "Abellino, the Bravo of Venice." They also read the novels of Walter Scott, Captain Marryatt, Bulwer, William and Mary Howitt, Miss Bremer, and (as soon as he appeared) Dickens. Harriet Beecher Stowe was at that time busy taking care of her children, and the great American novel was not yet born.

The factory girls were also omnivorous readers of the daily and weekly newspapers. From an article on this phase of the subject in the *Offering* — "Our Household," I am able to quote a sketch of one factory boarding-house "interior." The author said,—"In our house there are eleven boarders, and thirteen in all the members of the family. I will class them according to their religious tenets as follows: Calvinist, Baptist, Unitarian, Congregational,

Catholic, Episcopalian, and Mormonite, one each; Universalist and Methodist, two each; Christian Baptist, three. Their reading is from the following sources:—They receive regularly fifteen newspapers and periodicals. These are, the *Boston Daily Times*, the *Herald of Freedom*, the *Signs of the Times* and the *Christian Herald*, two copies each; the *Christian Register*, *Vox Populi*, *Literary Souvenir*, *Boston Pilot*, *Young Catholic's Friend*, *Star of Bethlehem* and the *Lowell Offering*, three copies each. A magazine [perhaps the *Dial*] one copy. We also borrow regularly the *Non Resistant*, the *Liberator*, the *Ladies' Book*, the *Ladies' Pearl* and the *Ladies' Companion*. We have also in the house what perhaps cannot be found anywhere else in the city of Lowell,—a Mormon Bible."

The names of the *Lowell Offering* writers, so far as I have been able to recall them are, as follows: Harriot F. Curtis and Harriet Farley, (the editors from 1842 to 1849), Harriet Lees, Lucy Larcom and Emeline Larcom, (sisters) Lura, Louisa and Maria Currier, (sisters), Margaret Foley, Lydia S. Hall, Sarah E. Martin, J. L. Baker, Abba Goddard, Harriet Jane Hanson, M. Bryant, Laura Tay, Jane S. Welch, Sarah Shedd, M. R. Green, Mary A. Leonard, Ellen M. Smith, M. A. Dodge, Caroline Whitney, E. W. Jennings, Betsey Chamberlain, Eliza J. Cate, A. H. Winship, Hannah Johnson, Mrs. Kimball, Adeline Bradley, L. A. Choate, A. E. Wilson, Sarah Bagley, Ann Carter, J. B. Hamilton, E. E. Turner, Hannah Johnson, A. D. Turner and Kate Clapp. Many of the writers signed fictious names,—such as Ella, Adelaide, Dorcas, Aramantha, Stella, Kate, Oriana, Ione, Annaline, and Ruth Rover. Lucy Larcom, M. Bryant, Harriet Farlev, Margaret Foley and Lydia S. Hall were the poets of the magazine. Lucy Larcom published her first poem in the *Offering*, in 1842. It was called "The River." It is almost superfluous to say that Miss Larcom and Miss Foley long since became celebrated: one as a poet, and the other as a sculptor of rare merit.

In her poem, "An Idyl of Work," Miss Larcom, in her most graceful and popular style tells the story of her life as a Lowell factory girl. Harriot F. Curtis was a prolific writer for newspapers and magazines under the pseudonyme of "Minnie Myrtle" (a *nom de plume* afterwards appropriated by a Mrs. Anna C. Johnson, for which see Wheeler's "Dictionary of Noted Names of Fiction." Miss Curtis published a book called "S. S. Philosophy," and two popular novels,—"Kate in Search of a Husband," and "Jessie's Flirtations." This last still holds its original place in the advertising list of Harper's Select Library of Novels. Harriet Farley wrote and published several books. Harriet J. Hanson Robinson published a book in 1877, "Warrington Pen Portraits." It is rumored that there are others of the *Offering* writers who have published books, but I have been unable so far to gather any reliable information on the subject.

Not many of the lesser lights continued to write after their contributions were no longer in demand for the *Offering*. Many of the writers graduated from the Lowell factories into other positions. A few went as missionaries to foreign countries. Some became teachers in Massachusetts and in other states. Here and there one became a minister, a physician or an artist. Lydia S. Hall, one of the most self-reliant among them, went out as a missionary to the Choctaws, and in "Border-Ruffian" days lived in Kansas. She afterwards went to Washington as clerk in the Treasury Department, and studied law at the same time.

Many of the Lowell factory girls made good "matches;" almost as good as if they had not worked for a living. They married men of all trades and professions, some of whom afterwards became Major Generals, Doctors of Divinity, and even members of Congress. These women as a rule made good wives and mothers, and they were not above doing their own housework and taking care of their children. Some of these children have added greatly to the business and mental stamina of their day and generation. A few of them, in education and true culture, have attained such excellence that they are worthy to be ranked with the children of the so-called Brahmin class in New England Society. The self-reliance taught in the hard school of factory life developed the characters of the mothers, and like good blood, *told* in the children, and helped to equip them to fight well the battle of life.

In 1849, the time foretold by one of the early writers of the *Lowell Offering* had come. She had said,—"Should the time arrive when the great congregation of operatives will cause a reduction of wages, the inducement to come here will be withdrawn." The great influx of the foreign element had caused this reduction, and changed entirely the tone of Lowell factory society. The class from which the *Offering* writers had been drawn, came no more to the "city of spindles," and the magazine became a thing of the past. No effort was ever made to repeat the experiment, and it would not have been successful if it had been made: since the class of operatives now employed in manufacturing towns and cities is so largely made up of the foreign element, whose traditions and tendencies are not quite in a literary direction,—to say the least. It was not so much individual as collective thought and aspiration, that made the Lowell *Offering* possible. The whole Lowell factory community in 1840 was filled with the idea of self-culture and a better education.

In order that the reader may understand the sort of people who composed this Arcadian settlement, it will be well to give a little sketch of it and its surroundings:—

Lowell, in 1835, was little more than a factory village. Help was in great demand, and fabulous stories were told of the new town (formerly Chelmsford) and the high wages offered to all classes of work-people; stories that reached the ears of mechanics and machinists in all parts of New England, and gave new life to lonely and dependent women in distant towns and farm houses. Into this Yankee El Dorado the needy people began to pour by the various modes of travel known to those old days. They came by the slow toiling canal, which then "tracked its sinuous way" from Boston to Lowell. This canal is no longer used, and there is nothing left of it but a little spot where it began in Charlestown. There, any one going by the Boston and Maine Railroad can see, just before reaching the Somerville station, a few decayed willows nodding sleepily over its grass-grown channel and ridgy paths,— a reminder of those slow times when it took a long summer's day to travel the twenty-eight miles from Boston to Lowell. The canal boat came every day, always filled with new recruits to the army of useful people. The mechanic and machinist came, each with his home-made tool chest, his household stuff, and his wife and little ones. The widow came with her little flock, and her scanty housekeeping goods, to open a boarding house or variety store, and so provide a home for her fatherless children. People with past histories came, to hide their griefs and their identity, and to earn an honest living by the "sweat of their brow." Single young men came, full of hope and life, to get money for an education, or to lift the mortgage from the home farm. Troops of young girls came by stages and baggage wagons, and men were employed to go into other states and Canada and collect them at so much a head and deliver them at the factories.

A very curious sight these country girls presented to young eyes accustomed to a more modern style of things. When the large covered baggage wagon arrived in front of a "block on the corporation" they would descend from it, dressed in various and outlandish fashions (some of the dresses, perhaps, having served for *best* during two generations) and with their arms brimfull of bandboxes containing all their worldly goods. These country girls, as they were called, had queer names, some of which added to the singularity of their appearance. Samantha, Triphena, Plumy, Elgardy, Leafy, Ruhamah, Lovey, and Florilla were among them. They soon learned the ways of the new place to which they had come, and after paying for their transportation they used their earnings to re-dress themselves, and in a little while were as stylish as the rest; for they had good New England blood in them, and blood tells even in factory people.

The Lowell factory girls were a simple folk. Many of them were young girls growing up in Arcadian simplicity; earning their bread and often that of others; working twelve hours a day, with three months schooling in a year, and eking out this scanty education with a little help from evening schools; reading such books as were found in the circulating libraries of the day; meeting for mutual improvement and help; striving to be good and to improve the mind; with minds wholly untroubled by conventionalities, or thoughts of class distinction; dressing simply, since they had no time to waste on ruffles or the entanglements of dress. Such were their lives. Undoubtedly there must have been another side of this picture, but the writer speaks of the side she knew best,—the bright side.

The *Lowell Offering* writers were of a little different class from those who came "down from the country." Some of them were daughters of professional men or teachers, whose mothers, left widows, were struggling to maintain the younger children. Some of them were the daughters of people in reduced circumstances, and had left home "on a visit" to send their wages surreptitiously in aid of the family purse. Some of them were the grand-daughters of patriots who had fought at Bunker Hill, and had lost the family means in the war for independence. There were a few who seemed to have mysterious antecedents, and to be hiding from something; and strange and distinguished looking men and women sometimes came to call upon them. Many farmer's daughters came from the neighboring towns to earn money to complete their wedding outfit, or buy the bride's share of housekeeping articles. But the most prevailing incentive to labor was to secure the means of education for some *male* member of the family. To

make a *gentleman* of a brother or a son, to give him a
college education, was the dominant thought in the minds
of a great many of the better class of operatives.   I have
known more than one young girl to give every cent of her
wages, month after month, to a brother, that he might get
the education necessary to enter some profession.   I have
known women to educate young men by their earnings, who
were not sons or relatives.   I have known a mother to work
years in this way for her boy.

These men, educated by the labor and self-sacrifice of
others, sometimes acquired just enough learning to make
them look down upon the social position in which their
women friends and relatives were still forced to remain.
The result to the recipient was often of doubtful value, so
far as the development of the affections was concerned.
Sometimes the great obligation was forgotten, and Lucy
Downing's pitiful story was again repeated in the experience of some lonely and neglected woman.   Only in rare
instances, to either party did the life-long result of such
sacrifice on the part of the women of the family become of
permanent and spiritual value !

The average woman of forty years ago was very humble
in her notions of the sphere of woman.   What if she did
hunger and thirst after knowledge?   She could do nothing
with it even if she could get it.   So she made a *fetich* of
some male relative, and gave him the mental food for which
she herself was starving; and devoted all her energies
towards helping him to become what she felt, under better
conditions, she herself might have been.   It was enough in
those early days to be the *mother* or *sister* of somebody.
Women were almost as abject in this particular as the
Thracian woman of old, who said:

> " I am not of the noble Grecian race,
> I'm poor Abrotonon, and born in Thrace;
> Let the Greek women scorn me, if they please,
> I was the mother of Themistocles."

There are women still left who believe their husbands,

sons, or male friends can study, read, and *vote* for them. They are like some frugal house-mothers, who think there is no need of a dinner if the goodman of the family is not coming home to share it. Just as if the man half of the human family can eat, " learn and inwardly digest," to make either physical or mental strength for the other half!

One word about the foreign element that crept in and destroyed the idyllic life of the Lowell factory operatives. The Englishman came first; the Irishman followed; but not until within a few years has the Frenchman, Italian and German come to take possession of the cotton mills. I remember very well the first foreigner who came to work on a certain Corporation. He brought with him his wife and a large family of boys and girls. The word poverty does not express the condition in which they first appeared before the eyes of the young Lowellians. Not one of the family wore shoes and stockings, or a covering for the head. The children did not look as if they had ever been introduced to a fine comb, or had made the acquaintance of soap and water. They were not clothed in a surplus of finery, and their brogue—who shall describe it? It was a mixture of the *patois* of the Cockney and the County Cork dialect. At first the whole family lived in a cellar, and people gave them food enough to keep souls and bodies together. The father was a blue-dyer, and soon got work. The mother took in washing, and one after another the children went into the factory. In ten years they owned a small house; and the girls in the family, in the enforced pauses of factory life,* had gone to school and learned to read and write a little. They dressed as well as other young persons of their age, and were fast making marriages suitable to their improved condition. The sons had been better educated: one had turned out to be an inventor, and another, the youngest, had been sent to college. I will not

---

* The authorities had made a law that all operatives under fourteen years of age should go to school three months in the year.

say what he became—only, that he now occupies a certain professional position. I often hear of him in public life. The other day he made a speech in which he expressed his opinion on the great question of equal rights. It was an opinion so common and so trite with a large class of our opposers, that I almost hesitate to repeat it. It was this:

"When the women show that they want to vote, I am willing to give them all the rights they want."

Give! I thought. Where did you get the right to *give* the Massachusetts women the right to vote? You did not inherit it. In what consists your prerogative over the women whose ancestors fought to secure the very right of suffrage of which you so glibly talk, and which neither you, nor your father before you, did aught to establish or maintain? Ah, old friend! If you had staid in your own country, you would have followed your father's trade, and would have had no more opportunity for education, or right to the ballot, than you are willing to give to the women. And your delicate hands, that in your eloquent perorations wave away so gracefully the rights of the daughters of your adopted State, would now and forever be indelibly stained with the ancestral tint of the blue-dye pot!

D.

THE FIRST NATIONAL WOMAN'S RIGHTS CONVENTION.

THE CALL.

"A Convention will be held at Worcester, Mass., on the 23rd and 24th of October next (agreeably to the appointment of a preliminary meeting held at Boston on the 30th of May last) to consider the question of WOMAN'S RIGHTS,

Duties, and Relations; and the Men and Women of our country, who feel sufficient interest in the great subject to give an earnest thought and effective effort to its rightful adjustment, are invited to meet each other in free conference, at the time and place appointed.

The upward-tending spirit of the age, busy in a hundred forms of effort for the world's redemption from the sins and sufferings which oppress it, has brought this one, which yields to none in importance and urgency, into distinguished prominence. One half of the race are its immediate objects, and the other half are as deeply involved, by that absolute unity of interest and destiny which nature has established between them.

The neighbor is near enough to involve every human being in a general equality of rights and community of interests; but Men and Women, in their reciprocities of love and duty, are one flesh and one blood—mother, wife, sister and daughter come so near the heart and mind of every man, that they must be either his blessing or his bane. Where there is such mutuality of interests, such an interlinking of life, there can be no real antagonism of position and action. The sexes should not, for any reason, or by any chance, take hostile attitudes toward each other, either in the apprehension or amendment of the wrongs which exist in their necessary relations; but they should harmonize in opinion and coöperate in effort, for the reason that they must unite in the ultimate achievement of the desired reformation.

Of the many points now under discussion and demanding a just settlement, the general question of Woman's Rights and Relations comprehends such as: Her Education, Literary, Scientific and Artistic; Her Avocations, Industrial, Commercial and Professional; Her Interests, Pecuniary, Civil and Political; in a word—her Rights as an individual, and her Functions as a Citizen.

No one will pretend that all these interests, embracing, as they do, all that is not merely animal in a human life, are rightly understood or justly provided for in the existing social order. Nor is it any more true that the constitutional differences of the sexes, which should determine, define and limit the resulting differences of office and duty, are adequately comprehended and practically observed.

Woman has been condemned, from her greater delicacy of physical organization, to inferiority of intellectual and moral culture, and to the forfeiture of great social, civil and religious privileges.. In the relation of marriage, she has been ideally annihilated, and actually enslaved in all that concerns her personal and pecuniary rights; and even in widowhood and single life, she is oppressed with such limitation and degradation of labor and avocation as clearly and cruelly mark the condition of a disabled caste. But, by the inspiration of the Almighty, the beneficent spirit of reform is roused to the redress of these wrongs. The tyranny which degrades and crushes wives and mothers, sits no longer lightly on the world's conscience— the heart's home-worship feels the stain of stooping at a dishonored altar. Manhood begins to feel the shame of muddying the springs from which it draws its highest life; and Womanhood is everywhere awakening to assert its divinely chartered rights, and to fulfil its noblest duties. It is the spirit of reviving truth and righteousness which has moved upon the great deep of the public heart, and aroused its redressing justice; and, through it, the Providence of God is vindicating the order and appointments of his creation.

The signs are encouraging; the time is opportune. Come, then, to this Convention. It is your duty, if you are worthy of your age and country. Give the help of your best thought to separate the light from the darkness. Wisely give the protection of your name and the benefit of your efforts to the great work of settling the principles, devising the method, and achieving the success of this high and holy movement."

The above call was signed in the following order:

MASSACHUSETTS.— Lucy Stone, William H. Channing, Harriot K. Hunt, A. Bronson Alcott, Nathaniel Barney, Eliza Barney, Wendell Phillips, Ann Greene Phillips, Adin Ballou, Anna Q. T. Parsons, Mary H. L. Cabot, B. S. Treanor, Mary M. Brooks, T. W. Higginson, Mary E. Higginson, Emily Winslow, R. Waldo Emerson, William Lloyd Garrison, Helen E. Garrison, Charles F. Hovey, Sarah Earle, Abby Kelley Foster, Dr. Seth Rogers, Eliza F. Taft, Dr. A. C. Taft, Charles K. Whipple, Mary Bullard, Emma C. Goodwin, Abby H. Price, Thankful Southwick, Eliza J. Kenney, Louisa M. Sewall, Sarah Southwick.

RHODE ISLAND.— Sarah H. Whitman, Thomas Davis, Paulina Wright Davis, Joseph A. Barker, Sarah Brown, Elizabeth B. Chace, Mary Clarke, John L. Clarke, George Clarke, Mary Adams, George Adams.

NEW YORK.— Gerrit Smith, Nancy Smith, Elizabeth Cady Stanton, Catharine Wilkinson, Samuel J. May, Charlotte C. May, Charlotte G. Coffin, Mary G. Taber, Elizabeth S. Miller, Elizabeth Russell, Stephen S. Smith, Rosa Smith, Joseph Savage, L. N. Fowler, Lydia Fowler, Sarah Smith, Charles D. Miller.

PENNSYLVANIA.— William Elder, Sarah Elder, Sarah' Tyndale, Warner Justice, Jane G. Swisshelm, Charlotte Darlington, Simon Barnard, Lucretià Mott, Myra Townsend, Mary Grew, Sarah Lewis, Sarah Pugh, Huldah Justice, William Swisshelm, James Mott, W. S. Pierce, Hannah Darlington, Sarah D. Barnard.

MARYLAND.— Eliza Stewart.

OHIO.— Elizabeth Wilson, Mary A. Johnson, Oliver Johnson, Mary Cowles, Maria L. Giddings, Jane Elizabeth Jones, Benjamin S. Jones, Lucius A. Hine, Sylvia Cornell.

OFFICERS OF THE CONVENTION.

President, Paulina W. Davis, of Rhode Island. *Vice Presidents*, William H. Channing, of Massachusetts, Sarah Tyndale, of Pennsylvania. *Secretaries*, Hannah M. Darlington, of Pennsylvania, Joseph C. Hathaway, of New York.

SPEAKERS IN THE CONVENTION.

Lucretia Mott, Abby H. Price, W. H. Channing, Ernestine L. Rose, Abby K. Foster, C. C. Burleigh, Wendell Phillips, J. N. Buffum, S. S. Foster, Harriot K. Hunt, Antoinette L. Brown, Mrs. Ball, W. A. Alcott, Sojourner Truth, A. Brown, Frederick Douglass, Wm. Lloyd Garrison, Sarah Tyndale, Martha H. Mowry, Lucy Stone.

LETTERS TO THE CONVENTION WERE RECEIVED FROM,

Elizabeth C. Stanton, Samuel J. May, L. A. Hine, Elizur Wright, O. S. Fowler, E. A. Lukens, Margaret Chappelsmith, Nancy M. Baird, Jane Cowen, Sophia L. Little, Elizabeth Wilson, Maria L. Varney, Mildred A. Spafard, H. M. Weber.

MEMBERS OF THE CONVENTION.

MASSACHUSETTS.— T. B. Elliot, Eliza J. Kenney, M. S. Firth, Julia A. McIntyre, Emily Sanford, H. M. Sanford, C. D. M. Lane, Elizabeth Firth, S. C. Sargeant C. A. K. Ball, M. A. Thompson, Lucinda Safford, S. E. Hall, S. D. Holmes, Z. W. Harlow, N. B. Spooner, Ignatius Sargent, A. B. Humphrey, M. R. Hadwen, J. H. Shaw, Olive Darling, M. A. Walden, A. P. B. Rawson, Nathaniel Barney, Sarah H. Earle, Lewis Ford, J. T. Everett, Loring Moody, Sojourner Truth, Rev. J. G. Forman, Andrew Stone, M. D., Samuel May. Jr., Sarah R. May, Charles Brigham, J. T. Partridge, Eliza C. Clapp, Daniel Steward, Sophia Foord, E. A. Clarke, E. H. Taft, Anna E. Ruggles, Mary Abbot, Anna E. Fish, C. G. Munyan, Maria L. Southwick, F. C. Johnson, Thomas Hill, Elizabeth Frail, Eli Belknap, M. M. Frail, Valentine Belknap, Effingham L. Capron, Frances H. Drake, E. M. Dodge, Eliza Barney, Lydia Barney, G. D. Williams, Elizabeth Earle, E. Jane Alden, Elizabeth Dayton, Lima H. Ober, Dorothy Whiting, Emily Whiting, Abigail Morgan, Mary R. Metcalf, R. H. Ober, D. A. Mundy, Dr. S. Rogers, Mrs. E. J. Henshaw, Edward Southwick, E. A. Merrick, Mrs. C. Merrick, C. S.

Dow, Josiah Henshaw, Andrew Wellington, Louisa Gleason, Paulina Gerry, Lucy Stone, Mrs. Chickery, Mrs. F. A. Pierce, C. M. Trenor, R. C. Capron, William Lloyd Garrison, Emily Loveland, Mrs. S. Worcester, Phebe Worcester, Adeline Worcester, Joanna R. Ballou, Abby H. Price, B. Willard, T. Pool, M. B. Kent, E. H. Knowlton, D. H. Knowlton, G. Valentine, A. Prince, Lydia Wilmarth, J. G. Warren, Mrs. E. A. Stowell, Martin Stowell, Mrs. E. Stamp, C. M. Barbour, Anna Q. T. Parsons, C. D. McLane, W. H. Channing, Wendell Phillips, Abby K. Foster, S. S. Foster, Wm. D. Cady, Mrs. J. G. Hodgden, C. M. Shaw, Ophelia D. Hill, Mrs. P. Allen, E. Goddard, M. F. Gilbert, A. H. Johnson, W. H. Harrington, E. B. Briggs, A. C. Lackey, Ora Ober, Thomas Provan, Rebecca Provan, A. W. Thayer, M. M. Munyan, W. H. Johnson, G. W. Benson, Mrs. C. M. Carter, H. S. Brigham, E. A. Welsh, Mrs. J. H. Moore, Margaret S. Merritt, Martha Willard, A. N. Lamb, Mrs. Chaplin, N. B. Hill, K. H. Parsons, C. Jillson, L. Wait, F. H. Underwood, J. B. Willard, Perry Joslin, Elizabeth Johnson, Seneth Smith, Marian Hill, Wm. Coe, E. T. Smith, S. Aldrich, M. A. Maynard, S. P. R., J. N. Cummings, Nancy Fay, M. Jane Davis, D. R. Crandell, E. M. Burleigh, Sarah Chafee, Adeline Perry, Lydia E. Chase, J. A. Fuller, Sarah Prentice, Emily Prentice, H. N. Fairbanks, Mrs. A. Crowl, Dwight Tracy, J. S. Perry, Isaac Norcross, E. A. Parrington, Mrs. Parrington, Harriot K. Hunt, Charles F. Hovey, Susan Fuller, Thomas Earle, Alice C. Earle, Martha B. Earle, Anne H. Southwick, Joseph A. Howland, Adeline H. Howland, O. T. Harris, Julia T. Harris, John M. Spear, E. D. Draper, D. R. P. Hewitt, L. G. Wilkins, J. H. Binney, Mary Adams, Anna Goulding, Olive W. Hastings.— 186.

CONNECTICUT.— C. M. Collins, A. H. Metcalf, Anna Cornell, S. Munroe, Anna E. Price, M. C. Munroe, Martha Smith, Lucius Holmes, Benj. Segur, Buel Picket, Lucy T. Dike, Asa Cutler, C. C. Burleigh, Gertrude R. Burleigh.

RHODE ISLAND.— Elizabeth B. Chace, Cynthia P. Bliss,

R. M. C. Capron, M. H. Mowry, Mary Eddy, Daniel Mitchell, Paulina W. Davis, G. Davis, A. Barnes, Dr. S. Mowry, Betsey F. Lawton.

VERMONT.—Mrs. A. E. Brown, Mrs. C. I. H. Nichols.

NEW HAMPSHIRE.— Sarah Pillsbury, P. B. Cogswell, Parker Pillsbury, Ira Foster, Julia Worcester.

MAINE.—Oliver Dennett, Anna R. Blake, Ellen M. Prescott.

NEW YORK.— Antoinette L. Brown, Pliny Sexton, Frederick Douglass, Edgar Hicks, J. C. Hathaway, Lucy N. Colman, Ernestine L. Rose, S. H. Hallock, Joseph Carpenter.

PENNSYLVANIA.—Hannah M. Darlington, Sarah Tyndale, Olive W. Hastings, Rebecca Plumley, S. L. Hastings, Janette Jackson, Anna R. Cox, Phebe Goodwin, Alice Jackson, Jacob Pierce, Lewis E. Capen, S. L. Miller, Isaac L. Miller, Lucretia Mott, Emma Parker.

OHIO.— Marian Blackwell, Ellen Blackwell, M. A. W. Johnson.

IOWA.—Silas Smith.

CALIFORNIA.— Mary G. Wright.

UNKNOWN.—Sophia Taft, Calvin Fairbanks, D. H. Knowlton, Alice H. Easton, E. W. K. Thompson, Mary R. Hubbard, E. J. Alden, Anna T. Draper, Josephine Reglar, Diana W. Ballou, Adeline S. Greene, Silence Bigelow, A. Wyman, L. H. Ober, Aseneth Fuller, Denney M. F. Walker, Eunice D. F. Pierce, Elijah Houghton.—82. Total, 268.

E.

HARRIOT K. HUNT'S PROTEST AGAINST TAXATION WITHOUT REPRESENTATION.

IN "Glances and Glimpses," a book published by Dr. Hunt in 1856, the writer gives her own experience at the time she was converted to the doctrine of "no taxation without representation." She says: "In October, 1851, when my taxes were to be paid, it was necessary for me to go to the Assessors' room that I might have some alteration made in the bill. While waiting there for this to be attended to, I received a lesson which thoroughly converted me to the belief that taxation without representation is a violation of human rights, and *there* I made up my mind to verify my theory by my practice. What so suddenly produced this effect? A pale, thin, waxy, tall, awkward, simple Irish boy, with that vacant stare which speaks of entire negation, and that shuffling manner indicating an errand-like aspect, brought into the Assessors' office a roll. It was near the time of an election, but I did not think of it. I said pleasantly, 'Is that paper to grant a naturalization?' I received a polite affirmative. 'Permit me to look at it?' 'Certainly.' There to my astonishment the above-described *gentleman* was invested with all the privileges of an American citizen. I query whether this Irish boy knew in what state Boston was located, whether in Massachusetts or Mississippi. This circumstance gave me an insight into the injustice of our laws forbidding women to vote, which decided me to pay my taxes next year under protest. Accordingly I sent the following protest:

To Frederick U. Tracy, Treasurer, and the Assessors, and other authorities of the City of Boston, and the citizens generally,

Harriot K. Hunt, physician, a native and permanent resident of the City of Boston, and for many years a tax payer therein, in making payment of her city taxes for the coming year, begs leave to protest against the injustice and inequality of levying taxes upon women, and at the same time refusing them any voice or vote in the imposition and expenditure of the same. The only classes of male persons required to pay taxes and not at the same time allowed the privilege of voting, are aliens and minors. The objection in the case of aliens, is, their supposed want of interest in our institutions, and knowledge of them. The objection in case of minors, is, the want of sufficient understanding. These objections certainly cannot apply to women, natives of the city, all whose property and interests are here, and who have accumulated by their own sagacity and industry the very property on which they are taxed. But this is not all; the alien by going through the forms of naturalization, the minor on coming of age, obtain the right of voting, and so long as they continue to pay a mere poll-tax of a dollar and a half, they may continue to exercise it, though so igno-rant as not to be able to *sign* their names, or *read* the very votes they put into the ballot boxes. Even drunkards, felons, idiots, or lunatics of *men*, may still enjoy that right of voting, to which no woman — however large the amount of taxes she pays, however respectable her character or useful her life — can ever attain. Wherein, your remon-strant would inquire, is the justice, equality, or wisdom of this?

That the rights and interests of the female part of the community are sometimes forgotten or disregarded in con-sequence of their deprivation of political rights, is strik-ingly evinced, as appears to your remonstrant, in the organization and administration of the city public schools. Though there are open in this State and neighborhood a great multitude of colleges and professional schools, for the education of boys and young men, yet the city has very properly provided two high schools of its own, one Latin, the other English, at which the *male graduates* of the grammar schools may pursue their education still further at the public expense, and why is not a like provision made for the girls? Why is the public provision for *their* educa-tion stopped short, just as they have attained the age best fitted for progress, and the preliminary knowledge neces-sary to facilitate it, thus giving the advantage of superior culture to *sex*, not to mind? The fact that our colleges and professional schools are closed against females, of which your remonstrant has had personal and painful experience—having been in the year 1847, after twelve years of medical practice in Boston, refused permission to attend the lectures of Harvard Medical College—that fact would seem to furnish an additional reason why the city should provide at its own expense those means of superior education, which, by supplying our girls with occupation and objects of interest, would not only save them from lives of frivolity and emptiness, but which might open the way to many useful and lucrative pursuits, and so raise them above that *degrading dependence,* so fruitful a source of female misery.

Reserving a more full exposition of the subject to future occasions, your remonstrant in paying her tax for the current year, begs leave to *protest* against the injustice and inequalities above pointed out.

This is respectfully submitted,

HARRIOT K. HUNT,
32 Green Street.

BOSTON, October 18, 1852.

The protest was copied in many American, as well as some English papers. It elicited inquiry, and many facts were brought to light illustrating the injustice of taxation without representation."

Dr. Hunt continued to protest every year as long as she lived, and her example was followed by women in Worcester, Plymouth, Lowell, Malden and perhaps in other places. No notice was taken of these protests by the proper authorities to whom they were addressed, but they served their purpose as a means of agitating the Woman's Rights question. The cry, "Taxation without representation is tyranny," has been ding-donged into the ears of the men of Massachusetts for the last thirty years. By and by, perhaps, they will begin to understand what it means.

F.

CONVENTIONS AND WOMEN'S MEETINGS HELD BY MRS. CAROLINE HEALEY DALL.

MRS. DALL'S connection with the early Woman's Rights movement in Massachusetts is very important. She held a successful Convention, (not mentioned in the text), June 1st, 1860, at the Meionaon, in Boston. Caroline M. Sevcrance presided, Samuel J. May, R. J. Hintin, Harriet Tubman, Rev. James Freeman Clark, Dr. Mercy B. Jackson, Elizabeth M. Powell, and Wendell Phillips, took part in the discussion. Theodore Parker had recently died in Florence, Italy, and Mrs. Dall made an able address on the work of his life. Mrs. E. D Cheney offered a resolution on the untimely death of this distinguished reformer. In the evening, Mrs. Dall spoke on the influence of law and literature upon the woman movement. So many women of position and culture had already become interested in this question, that this Convention may be called the most aristocratic meeting of the kind held up to that date. Previous to 1860, Mrs. Dall had given a course of twelve lectures in Boston, on the various phases of woman's rights. In them she claimed: 1. Woman's right to civil position. 2. Woman's right to higher education. 3. Woman's right to choice of vocation. 4. Woman's right to self-protection in the elective franchise. A *resumé* of these lectures was published in 1868, in book form, called "The College, the Market, and the Court."

Mrs. Dall's writings did a good work in forming public opinion, and creating interest on the subjects of which she treated. Some of the doctrines she taught had never before been publicly presented to Boston audiences. Her fresh and untrammelled thought was like seed-grain, and it was planted deep, to spring up and bear fruit for the increase of the woman's rights agitation. She made many distinguished converts. On her own authority it may be stated that she presided at the meeting when Ralph Waldo Emerson gave in his adherence to the Woman Suffrage Cause. Considering the early date of Mrs. Dall's labors in this direction, it is not too much to say, that her influence was of so great value that her name deserves to be recorded with those of Mary Wollstonecraft and Margaret Fuller.

Through her special efforts women were first put on the board of Officers of the American and the Boston Social Science Associations, and the result of this action vindicated at once and forever woman's fitness to occupy the same position in all public societies and associations, that man had hitherto claimed for himself alone. Since 1865 the American Social Science Association has admitted women to a position of entire equality, as members, officers, and as speakers at its annual conventions. This has been of great benefit, since it has encouraged women to express themselves in the presence of the wisest men, and enabled them to present to the public the woman side of some great questions.

G.

THREE MIDDLESEX COUNTY CONVENTIONS.

In 1875 three important woman suffrage conventions were held by the Middlesex County Woman Suffrage Association in the towns of Malden, Melrose and Concord. These meetings were conducted something after the style of local church conferences. They were well advertised, and many people came to them. A collation was provided by the ladies of each town, and the feast of reason was so judiciously mingled with the triumphs of cookery, that converting to the cause was never done so easily and so harmoniously. Many women present at one or the other of these conventions, said to the president: "I never before heard a woman's rights speech. If these are the reasons why women should vote, I believe in voting. I never thought of the subject in that light before."

At the Malden convention speeches were made by Mrs. Julia Ward Howe, Mrs. Lucy Stone, Miss Mary F. Eastman, Miss Huldah B. Loud, Henry B. Blackwell, Rev. George H. Vibbert, Rev. S. W. Bush, Rev. D. M. Wilson, and the president of the association, Mrs. Harriet H. Robinson. Letters were received from William Lloyd Garrison, Elizur Wright, Richard P. Hallowell, Bishop Gilbert Haven, Judge Robert C. Pitman, Hon. George F. Hoar and Mrs. Mary A. Livermore. An able set of resolutions, prepared by W. S. Robinson ("Warrington") was adopted:

Resolved, That Woman has an equal right with man to the ballot, and that to deprive her of the use of it is an act of usurpation which ought to be immediately discontinued.

Resolved, That we care not whether the right of Suffrage be called natural and absolute, or conventional, or dependent on capacity, or property, or on any kind of qualification which may be acquired, it is the same in woman as in man; that historically and legally — by Genesis and by the Statutes, this equality is specially recognized.

Resolved, That the reasons why women were excluded from voting at certain elections (not at all) and upon certain subjects (not upon all) by the framers of the Constitution, are no longer applicable; because, since the year 1780, woman has, in hundreds of instances, individually and in classes, broken over those restraints which were once held to keep her in subordinate positions in the active affairs of life; she teaches, preaches, practices the medical profession, edits newspapers, buys and sells, owns and manages property, and transacts business of all descriptions. The reason for the exclusion of Woman from the Suffrage having vanished, let the spirit and practice of exclusion go with it.

Resolved, That the pretense that Woman should be kept from the ballot-box and the town meeting, because government is founded upon force and military power, is a legal and historical falsehood, inasmuch as the Constitution, by Art. x, Sec. 1, Chap. 11, specifies a certain class of elections for the militia alone to share in; and as, furthermore, to confine the Suffrage to those who form the military force would exclude from our elections thousands of males who now vote, or who are now specially complained of for not voting; and finally because by the last and perhaps most important of the Declarations of Rights, it is stipulated that the power of making the laws and the power of executing them shall be kept forever apart, to the end that "it may be a government of laws and not of men."

Resolved, That the Legislature of Massachusetts, by persisting in its opposition to the granting of all petitions for the removal of usurping rules and statutes on the subject, is unjust; and that, no matter whether this spirit and practice of injustice be the result of carelessness or ignorance or malice, it is its duty at once to correct it, and no longer to interpose its own will and wilfulness against the demand of justice and the dictates of duty.

THE MELROSE CONVENTION

Was honored by the presence of Julia E. and Abby H. Smith of Glastonbury, Connecticut. These ladies, who have become famous, because of their resistance to the tyranny of " taxation without representation," told the story of their oppression in the most simple and effective manner. They stood upon the platform, (two gray-haired, sweet-faced ladies, both over seventy years of age, dressed just alike), and were introduced to the large audience. They remained standing; and while one read her carefully-prepared little speech, the other stood near and nodded approval, and, at the right time, reminded her sister of any little point about the sale of the cows that she had omitted, with " Don't you remember, Abby, that he was real rough to Whitey?" or "He said it much stronger than that, Abby." The story they told is as follows:

Julia E. Smith said: "These two women who have caused such a turmoil in their native place, and who have, as their opponents say, signally disgraced the ancient town of Glastonbury, Ct., now present themselves before you. What have we done? We have merely asserted that it is as wrong to take a woman's property without her consent, as it is to take a man's property without his consent; and we stand to it.

"No man or woman denies this in conversation. For this we have had our pet cows seized and sold at the auction block, our whole meadow land attached, and eleven acres sold for a tax of not quite fifty dollars, worth more than two thousand dollars. For this unlawful deed we tried to get redress, and a prominent and upright citizen of our own town decided in our favor, according to the statute which expressly declares that real estate cannot be taken where personal estate can be found. But these unjust men appealed to the Hartford Court of Common Pleas, and brought us up for three days in the severity of winter, seven miles from our dwelling, and told us that Mr. Briscoe, the regular judge, was sick and we must be tried by George G. Sumner, the City Judge. This was wholly false, for Judge Briscoe was hearing another case in the same building, and came in, the second day, and conversed with us. The judge took care to defer his decision two weeks and two days, so that it might be too late to bring the case before the court of errors for the March session, and then promised Mr. Cornwall. our lawyer, to give him the facts in the case. Mr. Cornwall has been obliged to sue the town, the collector and Hardin who has a deed of the meadow land, to bring up the case· before the Court of Equity to set aside the deed, and the Court has appointed a committee to take cognizance of the business. But Goslee, the town lawyer, objects to every one, and the Court will be obliged to appoint men of their own choice. The whole iniquity has been concocted beforehand, and their contrivance is, for our old enemy to record his deed before the year is up.

Our lawyer seems to think that all this affair is so unlawful that there is no danger in letting it go over the year. But that we are not willing to suffer, for we cannot bear to see all our hay hauled up through our yard directly by the house for the advantage of such an ugly neighbor, and we do not see that it can aid the Suffrage cause to throw away, and worse than throw away, two or three thousand dollars, to our unspeakable injury. Did our forefathers pass through a seven years' bloody war, that only half their posterity should be benefited by the sacrifice and be left without appeal either to town or state? The state took no notice of our petition (there being no discussion upon it) except to give us leave to withdraw; all the privilege we ever have had from its laws. We seem to be left without a country, and we cannot see but we should fare better under a king; for King George himself never attached woman's property in so unfeeling and cowardly a manner as has been done to us. He merely tried to collect some duties of his subjects, and they had the privilege of refraining from drinking a cup of tea, which many of the women were brave enough to do a hundred years ago. Now men propose to celebrate their victory over taxation without representation by keeping a grand Centennial, while they leave half their citizens in a situation to suffer the same tyranny. We have now another tax hanging over our heads, of 150 dollars, sent us by mail last October, which they do not at present venture to collect, as has been intimated to us, until the next session of the Legislature, when they will get an *ex post facto* law passed, as they have done before, to sanction their illegal doings. It may therefore be possible we shall have a furnished house to receive our friends in, till next June."

These two solitary women, who have not a relative to defend them, seem to stand on so firm a foundation that it requires, to put them down, a whole State and all the authority of a town, who break their own laws, silence the newspapers from speaking of them, change the regular court judge, and no doubt will pass new State laws against them; yet they have not succeeded in moving them from their stronghold.

The cows of the Smith sisters were all sold to pay the taxes on property owned by them, and the town authorities began to sell their land piecemeal. Julia's account of the sale of the cows is told in the introduction to her pamphlet on the subject. There were seven cows in all, at the first sale at the sign-post. Of these, three were afterwards disposed of. The four others, "Daisy, Whitey, Minnie and Proxy, with one other, have been driven to be sold at the auction-block, this centennial year." A calf belonging to Proxy, came while the mother was shut up for a forced sale at the sign-post, and was named Martha Washington. Another calf that came about the same time to Whitey, was called Abigail Adams.*

The new speakers at the Melrose convention, were Hon. Samuel E. Sewall and Mrs. Mary A. Livermore.

THE CONCORD CONVENTION

Was held about a month after the great Centennial Celebration of April 19, 1875, — a celebration in which no woman belonging to that town took any official part. Nor was there any place of honor found for the more distinguished women who had come long distances to share in the festivities of the day. Some of the women present were descendents of John Hancock, of Benjamin Franklin, of Ezra Ripley, of Samuel Prescott, of Thomas Emerson, and of John Cogswell.

---

* Retribution followed fast in the track of the town officer who sold the cows. In January, 1881, Julia E. Smith, in a letter to the *Woman's Journal*, says,— " The old Collector, Albert Crane, by whom our cows have been seized and driven to the sign-post five times, was not re-elected, as the Republicans carried the day. It was found the town is likely to lose some thousands of dollars by him. He avers that some one stole his Collector's book at the last town-meeting, and he cannot settle with the town. I cannot tell who believes it. I am not surprised at anything he says."

Though no seat of honor in the big tent in which the speeches were made was given to the women of to-day—silent memorials of those who had taken part in the events of one hundred years ago, had found a conspicuous place there—the scissors that cut the immortal cartridges made by the women on that eventful day, and the ancient flag that the fingers of some of the mothers of the Revolution had made. Though the Concord women were not permitted to share the Centennial honors, they were not deprived of the privilege of paying their part of the expenses incident to the occasion. To meet these, an increased tax-rate was assessed upon all the property owners in the town; and, since one-fifth of the town tax of Concord is paid by women, it will be easy to estimate this part of their share in the great Centennial celebration of 1876.

The knowledge of the proceedings at Concord added new zest to the spirit of the three conventions, and the events of the day were used by the speakers to point the moral of the Women's Rights question. Lucy Stone made one of her most effective and eloquent speeches upon this subject. She said:

"Fellow citizens (I had almost said fellow subjects) What we need is that women should feel their mean position; when that happens, they will soon make an effort to get out of it. Everything is possible to him that wills. All that is needed for the success of the cause of woman suffrage is to have women know that they want to vote. The law in this State classes women, children, idiots and criminals together, because those four classes are not allowed to vote. Concord and Lexington got into a fight about the Centennial, and Concord voted $10,000 for the celebration in order to eclipse Lexington. One-fifth of the tax of Concord is paid by the women, yet not one of these women dared to go to the Town Hall and cast her vote upon that subject. This is exactly the same thing which took place one hundred years ago, taxation without representation, against which the *men* of Concord then rebelled.

15

If I were an inhabitant of Concord, I would let my house be sold over my head and my clothes off my back and be hung by the neck before I would pay a cent of it!

Men of Melrose, Concord and Malden, why persecute us? Would you like to be a slave? Would you like to be disfranchised? Would you like to be bound to respect the laws which you cannot make? There are fifteen millions of women whom the Government denies legal rights. The consent of the governed is necessary to a just government. Women are governed, therefore they should have a vote in government. Jeff. Davis was deprived of his right to vote. What have the women of America done that Jeff. Davis should be their peer? Year after year we have been to the State House and pleaded our cause; this year the committee listened to us and gave us a good report, but we were voted down without a word in our defence in the Senate, and only secured a small vote in the House. Half an hour was spent on this vital subject, and the members spent four times that length of time on considering the size of a "barrel of cranberries"; that subject they were capable of grasping. Women, rally together and select and send to Congress and the Legislature the men who have helped you and will truly represent you."

Mrs. Stone then traced the gradual advancement of women from a state of legal and social degradation to their present position, and exhorted the women to learn to fight for their rights both by argument and persuasion; and ended thus:

> "The fault, dear [sisters], is not in our stars,
> But in ourselves, that we are underlings."

The Concord Convention was well attended; and among the speakers were many of those who had addressed the Malden and Melrose conventions. The new speakers were Ralph Waldo Emerson, A. Bronson Alcott, and Elizabeth K. Churchill.

The experience of the Concord women at the Centennial

celebration was well told by Miss Louisa M. Alcott in a newspaper article written at the time, and was much commented on by the press. To people who only knew the town by its great reputation as a literary centre, or as the place from which the first and longest shot was fired for freedom, (immortalized in Mr. Emerson's verse), such a transaction seemed hardly credible. It might be supposed that a spot upon which the battle for freedom and independence was first begun, would always be the vantage ground of questions relating to personal liberty. But such is not the fact. For instance, Concord was never an anti-slavery town, though some of its best citizens took active part in all the abolition movements. When the time came that women were allowed to vote for school committees, the same intolerant spirit which ignored and shut them out of the Centennial celebration was again manifested toward them, —not only by the leading magnates but also by the petty officials of the town. Some of these have from the first shown a great deal of ingenuity in inventing ways to intimidate and mislead the women voters. The men voters are not to blame for this state of things in their town, except that they do not take interest enough in the matter to insist that the women voters shall be fairly and respectfully treated.

The town of Concord has been crowned with many well-deserved honors.

" Tis true,
And pity 'tis, 'tis true,"

that to these honors must be added this unenviable distinction,—that it is the banner town for snubbing women voters !

H.

THE WOMAN SUFFRAGE COMMEMORATIVE CONVENTION IN 1880.

AT its annual meeting in May 1880, the Massachusetts Woman Suffrage Association voted to hold a Woman Suffrage Jubilee Convention, and chose the following named persons as a committee of arrangements; Lucy Stone, Abby Kelley Foster, Thomas J. Lothrop, Timothy K. Earle, Sarah E. Wall, Harriet H. Robinson and E. H. Church.

Members of this committee made the necessary arrangements, and at the appointed time the friends gathered at Worcester. There were present not only old workers, but also young and ardent suffragists, who had come to see those whose silver hairs told of long and faithful service. Athol, Boston, Haverhill, Leicester, Leominster, Lowell, Malden, Melrose, Milford, North Brookfield, Taunton, and many other Massachusetts towns were well represented. Suffragists from other states were also there, and letters were read from far away old friends, and those near, who were unable to be present. The oldest ladies there were Mrs. Lydia Brown of Lynn, Mrs. Wilbour of Worcester, and Julia E. Smith Parker of Glastonbury, Connecticut. On the afternoon of the first day there was an informal gathering of friends in the ante-room of Horticultural Hall in Worcester, and the congratulations and glad recognition of old acquaintances were very pleasant to behold. Old time memories were recalled by those who had not seen each other for many years, and the common salutation was: "How gray you've grown!" Many of them had indeed grown gray in the service, and their faces were changed, but made beautiful by a life devoted to a noble purpose.

There were many present who had attended the convention of thirty years ago. Abby Kelley Foster, Lucy Stone, Antoinette Brown Blackwell, Paulina Gerry (whose careful preservation of Woman's Rights documents has made the writing of this history possible), Dr. Martha H. Mowry, Rev. Samuel May, Rev. W. H. Channing, Joseph A. Howland, Adeline H. Howland and many, many others. It was very pleasant indeed to hear these veterans, whose clear voices have spoken out so long and so bravely for the cause,—William H. Channing, who, fresh from England, brought the good word concerning the movement in the mother country; Lucy Stone, whose "silvery voice" rose just as it did thirty years ago, and whose heart, as of old, was young and "warm with enthusiasm" for woman's rights; Antoinette Brown Blackwell, still "beautiful" and "orthodox;" and Samuel May, always effective in speech, and on the right side in *all* reforms.

Abby Kelley Foster too was there, feeble with declining years, but ever the "gentle hero," with the old fire of anti-slavery times still burning within her. In one part of her speech she had accused the men of being to blame for the political disfranchisement of women; and, turning suddenly to Mr. T. W. Higginson, (who sat near her on the platform) she shook her finger at him and said: "*You* are my enslaver!" Mr. Higginson took the accusation cheerfully, and the audience were delighted at the little scene. It reminded some of the more belligerent among them of the early times in the history of the cause, when the "fight" in Massachusetts was more aggressive than it has since become. The speaking at all the sessions was excellent, and the spirit of the Convention was very reverent and hopeful.

The tone of the press concerning woman's rights meetings had changed greatly since thirty years ago. "Hen conventions" had gone by, and a woman's meeting was now called by its proper name. Representatives of leading newspapers from all parts of the State were present, and the reports were written in a most just and friendly spirit. The Worcester press was particularly hospitable, and advertised the meetings gratuitously. The *Spy* said: "The convention is one of the best the women have ever held in Worcester."

I.

SUMMARY OF VOTING LAWS RELATING TO WOMEN, FROM 1691 TO 1822.

PROVINCE Charter, A. D. 1691, 3d year of William and Mary.—" The great and general Court shall consist of the Governor and Council (or assistants for the time being) and of such freeholders as shall be, from time to time, elected or deputed by the major part of the freeholders and other inhabitants of the respective towns or places, who shall be present at such elections."

Constitution, 1820, Part II, Chap. I, Sect. II, Art. II, gives the right of voting for Senators and Councillors to every *male* inhabitant 21 years of age, having a freehold estate *in the Commonwealth* of the annual income of £3, or any estate of the value of £60.* (Motion in Constitutional Convention to strike out the word *male*).

Constitution, Part II, Chap. I, Sect. III. Art. IV.—Qualification for a voter for Representatives, varies from the above by requiring that the voter shall own a freehold estate within the town where he resides. (Motion in Constitutional Convention to strike out the word *male*).

Constitution, Part II, Chap. 2, Sect. I, Art. III, also Sect. II. Art. I.—The persons who can vote for Senators or Representatives, can vote for Governor and Lieut. Governor. (Motion in Constitutional Convention to strike out the word *male*).

Constitution, Part II, Chap. I, Sect. I, Art. IV.—The Legislature has power to name and settle annually, or provide by fixed laws for the naming and settling, all civil officers within said Commonwealth, the election and constitution of whom are not hereafter in this form of government otherwise provided.

By Statute, 1785, Chap. 75, Sect. II, passed March 23,

* Property representation for Senators was abolished in 1840.

1786.—Town officers are to be chosen by the freeholders and other inhabitants of each town who shall pay to one single tax, *besides the poll-tax*, a sum equal to two-thirds of a single poll-tax. The selectmen are only required to be inhabitants of the town—not required to be voters.

Statute, 1809, Chap. 25, Sects. II. and III., allows *any persons* who are inhabitants of the towns, and citizens of the United States, who have paid taxes within a town for two years, to vote for town officers.

Statute, 1809, Chap. 39, repeals the foregoing.

Statute, 1811, Chap. 9, Sect. I., allows every *male* citizen of the Commonwealth, 21 years of age, liable to be taxed, who has resided one year in any town, to vote in the election of all town officers.

Constitutional Amendment, 1820.—Regulates the right of voting for Governor, Representatives, etc.

Statute, 1822, Chap. 104, Sect. I.—The same regulation was adopted in regard to voting at town meetings, as in regard to all other State officers.

SUMMARY.

1. Women were not excluded from voting from 1691 to 1780.

2. Women were excluded from voting only for certain offices from 1780 to 1785.

3. Three distinct sets of qualifications for voting till 1820.

4. Two distinct sets of qualifications for voting till 1822.

5. Qualifications for voting for town officers *more liberal* than for Governor and Legislature.

6. Qualifications for voting for *all* State, county and town officers, were first made uniform by Statute in 1822, and may be again enlarged by Statute, except where specified in the Constitution.

J.

EARLY LEGISLATIVE HEARINGS ON WOMAN'S RIGHTS. MARY U. FERRIN. REV. OLYMPIA BROWN.

THE first Hearing on the question of woman's rights in Massachusetts, so far as I have been able to learn, was before the Committee on the Qualifications of Voters, of the Constitutional Convention, June 3, 1853. This Hearing was held in answer to the 2,000 petitioners, who had asked for the recognition of woman's legal and property rights in the proposed amendments to the Constitution of the state. The Committee was addressed by Lucy Stone, Theodore Parker, Wendell Phillips and Thomas W. Higginson. An appeal to the citizens of Massachusetts, from the petitioners, had been issued in April 1853, in which woman's right to property and political equality was ably presented. This appeal was signed by Abby May Alcott, Abby Kelley Foster, Lucy Stone, Thomas W. Higginson, Anne Greene Phillips, Wendell Phillips, Anna Q. T. Parsons, Theodore Parker, William I. Bowditch, Samuel E. Sewall, Ellis Gray Loring, Charles K. Whipple, William Lloyd Garrison, Harriot K. Hunt, Thomas T. Stone, John W. Browne, Francis Jackson, Josiah F. Flagg, Mary Flagg, Elizabeth Smith, Eliza Barney, Abby H. Price, William C. Nell, Samuel May Jr., Robert F. Walcott, Robert Morris and A. Bronson Alcott.*

In 1857 a Hearing was held before the Committee on the Judiciary of the Massachusetts Legislature to listen to

---

* From the *Una*, a woman's paper published in Providence, R. I., in 1853. The editor of this paper was Paulina Wright Davis. Its chief contributor was Elizabeth Cady Stanton. Among its correspondents were Caroline H. Dall, Lucy Stone, Elizabeth P. Peabody, Thomas W. Higginson, Ednah D. Cheney and other Massachusetts writers. See "The History of Woman Suffrage." Stanton, Anthony, and Gage, Editors. New York: Fowler and Wells.

arguments in favor of the petition of Lucy Stone and others for equal property rights for women and for the "right of suffrage." The Representatives' Hall was well filled with interested listeners; Rev. James Freeman Clarke, Wendell Phillips and Lucy Stone made eloquent speeches.

Another Hearing was held in the same place in February, 1858, before the Joint Special Committee on the Qualifications of Voters. In one of "Warrington's" letters to the *New York Tribune* the following account of this Hearing is given: "Among the speakers were Mr. Phillips, Mr. Samuel E Sewall, Harriot K. Hunt, M. D., and others. The Committee aforesaid were giving a hearing to the petitioners for the extension of the right of suffrage to women. One of the petitioners is Sarah E. Wall of Worcester, who, like Dr. Hunt and Lucy Stone, is a 'taxpayer,' and who now petitions the Legislature, as she says, 'for the third and last time,' in behalf of the great principle that taxation and representation are inseparable. She argues the question, and winds up by saying:

'We do not expect to remedy all the evils of society, or that the defects of woman will be speedily corrected; she will commit her follies still, as man does; she will sometimes make a mistake in voting, as many wise men have done; but with all her follies, and all her mistakes, she cannot possibly bring on the country a more perverted state of the moral atmosphere than the present, or a worse financial crisis than that through which we are now passing. We do not send our petitions to you year after year, merely for you to report "leave to withdraw;" we demand action, immediate action. If it cannot be done in the name of affection, in the name of justice it *must* be done. If, in the absence of every argument, after the removal of every objection, you still persist in refusing her appeal, but one step remains for her to take, and that is, to refuse to pay taxes, and she will do it.'

Dr. Hunt gave the Committee, and the men generally, a

'piece of her mind' on the subjects of taxation, education, voting, tobacco, sending silly boys to College and
making sensible girls fold their hands in despair at home,
and so on. In reply to a question by the Chairman, as to
the reason why so few women had asked for the right of
suffrage, she made the pertinent inquiry, if women who
were choked could be expected to breathe?'

Mr. Phillips, in opening his speech, said woman's influence ought to be recognized. She exerts her due share of
power, but this power is irresponsible. All unseen power
is dangerous. The whole question was in fact yielded
when the schools were opened. The Turk says, woman
has no soul; books, thoughts, do not belong to her; they
keep her in the harem. But Western Europe recognizes
her mind, but it there stops at an artificial barrier. Men
were so stopped when they asked to be allowed to vote,
and the struggle is now going on for that right. We ask
you to reform symmetrically. Voting follows property.
When property went to the middle classes, they overthrew
the thrones. Our fathers said women should not have
property. But all this is changed. When you made the
change in the laws as to property, you granted all that we
asked. Do you say that woman has not sufficient ability to
vote? You don't vote on ability. Webster has not a
hundred votes and the inferior man one. All are alike.
If woman has ability enough to entitle her to be tried, and
to be sent to prison, she has ability enough to vote. If she
has not ability enough to make laws, she has not enough
to be punished for breaking them.

Brougham has said, within a year, that the legislation of
England in relation to woman is a disgrace to the statute-
book of any country. We don't care what woman's ability
is; we cannot know until the field is opened to her. She
has the same qualities of mind as large classes of men. So
long as government takes from woman a part of her labor
in taxes, it is bound to place in her hands the ballot. There
is no ground of opposition to this claim but the ground of

sex. But the Constitution is not based on sex. Every act of legislation for twenty years goes to break down this distinction. When woman has a ballot, the selfishness of the world will recognize and educate her; wealth will hasten to make her intelligent for its own security. Then when she wants to enter some new field of toil she can do so. Recognized as a voter, she can go anywhere. Look at the question of the vice of cities. How can you reach it while woman is under the foot of man? You confine her to the mill or the shop; you starve her by competition; and when the crisis comes 40,000 women seek the pavements with no bread, and then men say they are licentious. But who is to blame? Let woman be a doctor, a lawyer, an engraver, a teacher, and she will be subject to no more competition than man. Then this vast mass of festering corruption will be taken gently away by the laws of trade and nature. We shall get this finally; step by step the reform goes forward; but we ask a symmetrical reform. The question is, how soon will you decently surrender? Give us leave to present the question to the people in their primary assemblies. You can't decide questions of intellect and races. The Constitution knows nothing of these things. It only recognizes sentient, tax-paying beings. It is the old question of the oppressed asking the oppressor to relinquish his power. The Jew asked it; the Dissenter asked it; the Chartist is asking it, and woman is here asking it. It is the last great protest of one half the human race against injustice. Mr. Phillips made a very beautiful speech. It was one of his easy, rivulet like efforts, which charm rather than thrill you."

A second Hearing on the right of suffrage for women was held the following week before the same committee. Thomas W. Higginson made an address and Caroline Healey Dall read an essay "which," wrote "Warrington," " was not only very eloquently written but, in which also, the question was very ably argued."

In 1858, Stephen A. Chase of Salem from the same

Committee, on the Qualifications of Voters, made a long report on the petitions which had been presented for extending the right of suffrage to women. This report closed with an order that the State Board of Education make inquiry and report to the next Legislature, "whether it is not practicable and expedient to provide by law some method by which the women of this State may have a more active part in the control and management of the schools." There is nothing in legislative records to show that the State Board of Education reported favorably. But the above statement shows that ten years before Samuel E. Sewall's petition on the subject, a movement was made towards making women legally "eligible to serve as members of School Committees."

Since 1849, when the first petition for woman suffrage was presented to the Legislature, a great deal of hard work had been done every year in circulating petitions for this cause. These petitions were usually carried about by women who went from house to house to get the names of signers; and they were often snubbed for their pains by their neighbors and townsmen, and hooted at as an "old woman's rights" by the boys in the streets. These devoted women did the drudgery, endured the hardships, and suffered the humiliations attendant upon the early history of our cause; but their names are forgotten, and we, the eleventh hour people, reap the benefit of their labors. These silent workers were so modest and so anxious for the success of their petitions, that they never put their own names at the head of the list, but rather secured that of some leading person, so that others seeing his name might be induced to follow his example. In legislative documents a petition is recorded as, "The petition of John Smith and [so many] others." Thus it happens that "John Smith," who perhaps cared very little about the thing petitioned for, is the only name to be found in the records, while "Mary Jones," who circulated the petition and is deeply interested in the cause it represents, is irretrievably lost among the "others."

Among the earliest of these silent workers for the woman's rights cause may be mentioned Mary Upton Ferrin. In the "History of Woman Suffrage" she is spoken of as follows "The first change in the tyrannous laws of Massachusetts was really due to the work of this one woman, Mary Upton Ferrin, who for six years, after her own quaint method, poured the hot shot of her earnest conviction of woman's wrongs into the Legislature. In circulating petitions, she travelled six hundred miles, two thirds of this distance on foot. Much money was expended besides her time and travel, and her name should be remembered as that of one of the brave pioneers of the work." Mrs. Ferrin's petitions were for a change in the laws concerning the property rights of married women, and for the political and legal rights of all women.

In 1849 she prepared a memorial to the Massachusetts Legislature in which are embodied many of the demands for woman's equality before the law, which have so often been made to that body since that time. This memorial was printed by order of the Legislature (Leg. Doc. Ho. 57) and is called, "Memorial of the female signers of the several petitions of Henry A. Hardy and others," presented March 1, 1849. The document is not signed, and Mrs. Ferrin's name is not found with it upon the records; neither does her name appear in the Journals of the House in connection with any of the petitions and addresses she caused to be presented to the Legislature of the State. For this reason, and because I had never heard of her name in connection with suffrage work, it unfortunately happens that it is not recorded in its proper place, in the text of this book. But for the loyal friendship of the few who knew of her work and were willing to give her due credit, the name of Mary Upton Ferrin and the memory of her labors would have gone with her into the "great darkness."

There may be other early workers whose names or record I have been unable to obtain, and I will say here, to those who read this book, that if they have facts worthy of preservation in connection with the early suffrage work in this State, I shall be glad to receive them and will preserve them for the use of future historians.

While writing these very lines I received a letter from Rev. Olympia Brown, containing the facts relating to the inception of the New England Woman Suffrage Association. Mrs. Brown writes:

"After my return from Kansas in '67, I felt that we ought to do something for the cause in Massachusetts. There was at that time no organization in the State, and there had been no revival of the subject in the minds of the people since the war, which had swallowed up every other interest. In the spring of '68, I wrote to Abby Kelley Foster, telling her my wish to have something done in our own State, and she advised me to call together a few persons known to be in favor of suffrage some day during anniversary week, in some parlor in Boston. I corresponded with Adin Ballou, E. D. Draper and others on the subject and talked the matter over with Prof. T. T. Leonard, teacher of elocution, who offered his hall for a place of meeting. I wrote a notice inviting all persons interested in woman suffrage to come to Mr. Leonard's Hall, on a certain day and hour. At the time appointed the hall was full of people. I opened the meeting, and stated why I had called it, others took up the theme, we had many impromptu speeches, and we had a lively meeting. All agreed that something should be done, and a committee of seven was appointed to call a convention for the purpose of organizing a woman suffrage association. Caroline M. Severance, Stephen S. Foster, Miss Southwick and myself, were of this committee. I do not remember the other names.

We held a number of meetings and finally decided to call a convention early in the autumn of 1868. This convention was held in Horticultural Hall, and the result was the organization of the New England Woman Suffrage Association."

K.

AN ACT TO GIVE WOMEN THE RIGHT TO VOTE FOR MEMBERS OF SCHOOL COMMITTEES.

Be it enacted, etc., as follows:

SECT. 1. Every woman who is a citizen of this Commonwealth, of twenty-one years of age and upwards, and has the educational qualifications required by the twentieth article of the amendments to the Constitution, excepting paupers and persons under guardianship, who shall have resided within this Commonwealth one year and within the city or town in which she claims the right to vote six months next preceding any meeting of citizens either in wards or in general meeting for municipal purposes, and who shall have paid by herself, or her parent, or guardian, a state or county tax, which within two years next preceding such meeting has been assessed upon her in any city or town, shall have a right to vote at such town or city meeting, for members of school committees.

SECT. 2. Any female citizen of this Commonwealth may, on or before the fifteenth day of September in any year, give notice in writing to the assessors of any city or town, accompanied by satisfactory evidence, that she was on the first day of May of that year an inhabitant thereof and that she desires to pay a poll tax and furnish under oath a true list of her estate, both real and personal, and she shall thereupon be assessed for her poll and estate, and the assessors shall, on or before the first day of October in each year, return her name to the clerk of the city or town in the list of the persons so assessed. The taxes so assessed shall be entered in the tax list of the collector of the city or town, and the collector shall collect and pay over the same in the manner specified in his warrant.

SECT. 3. All laws in relation to the registration of voters shall apply to women upon whom the right to vote is herein conferred, provided that the names of such women shall be placed on a separate list.

SECT. 4. The mayor and aldermen of cities and the selectmen of towns may in their discretion appoint and notify a separate day for the election of school committees: *provided*, that such meeting shall be held in the same month in which the annual town meeting or the municipal election occurs. [*Approved April 16, 1879.*]

THE ACT AS AMENDED IN 1881.

Be it enacted etc., as follows ·

SECT. 1. Every woman who is a citizen of this Commonwealth, of twenty-one years of age and upwards, and has the educational qualifications required by the twentieth article of the amendments to the Constitution, excepting paupers and persons under guardianship, who shall have resided within this Commonwealth one year, and within the city or town in which she claims the right to vote six months next preceding any meeting of citizens, either in wards or in general meeting for municipal purposes, and who shall have paid, by herself, or her parent, guardian, or trustee, a state, county, city, or town tax which, within two years next preceding such meeting has been assessed upon her or her trustees, in any city or town, shall have a right to vote, at such town or city meeting, for members of school committees.

SECT. 2. Any woman who is a citizen of this Commonwealth may, on or before the first day of October in any year, give notice in writing to the assessors of any city or town, accompanied by satisfactory evidence, that she was, on the first of May of that year, an inhabitant thereof, and that she desires to pay a poll tax, and furnish, under oath, a true list of her estate, both real and personal, not exempt from taxation, and she shall thereupon be assessed for her poll, not exceeding fifty cents, and for her estate; and the assessors shall, on or before the fifth day of October, in each year, return her name to the clerk of the city or town in the list of the persons so assessed. The taxes so assessed shall be entered in the tax-list of the collector of the city or town, and the collector shall collect and pay over the same in the manner specified in his warrant.

SECT. 3. All laws in relation to the registration of voters shall apply to women upon whom the right to vote is herein conferred; *provided*, that the names of such women may be placed upon a separate list, and when the name of any woman has been placed on the voting list of any city or town, it shall continue on the list of said city or town as long as she continues to reside there, and to pay any state or county, city, or town tax that has been assessed on her or her trustee in any city or town in the Commonwealth within two years previous to any voting day.

SECT. 4. All acts and parts of acts inconsistent here-with are hereby repealed.

SECT. 5. This act shall take effect upon its passage.

L.

THREE DECISIONS OF THE SUPREME JUDICIAL COURT OF MASSACHUSETTS AGAINST THE RIGHTS OF THE WOMEN OF THE COMMON WEALTH.

THE first decision was in the case of Sarah E. Wall of Worcester, who had refused to pay her taxes under the following protest:

" Believing with the immortal Declaration of Independence that taxation and representation are inseparable; believing that the Constitution of the State furnishes no authority for the taxation of woman; believing also that the Constitution of the higher law of God, written on the human soul, requires us, if we would be worthy the rich inheritance of the past and true to ourselves and the future, to yield obedience to no statute that shall tend to fetter its aspirations, I shall henceforth pay no taxes until the word *male* is stricken from the voting clauses of the Constitution of Massachusetts.

SARAH E. WALL.

Worcester Daily Spy, Oct. 5. 1858.

Miss Wall was prosecuted by the city collector, and she carried her case before the Supreme Court, where she appeared for herself, W. A. Williams appearing for the collector. In a written account of this matter in 1881, Miss Wall says: "Although it was in 1858 that my resistance to taxation commenced, it was not until 1863 that the contest terminated and the decision was rendered. I think the Supreme Court would always find some way to evade a decision on this question."

"Wheeler *vs.* Wall, 6 Allen, 558.

"By the Constitution of Massachusetts, c. 1, § 1, article 4, the Legislature has power to impose taxes upon all the inhabitants of and persons resident, and estates lying within the said Commonwealth. By the laws passed by the Legislature in pursuance of this power and authority, the defendant is liable to taxation, although she is not qualified to vote for the officers by whom the taxes were assessed.

"The Court, acting under the Constitution, and bound to support it and maintain its provisions faithfully, cannot declare null and void a statute which has been passed by the Legislature, in pursuance of an express authority conferred by the Constitution." (Opinion by the Chief Justice, George Tyler Bigelow).

The second decision on the will of Francis Jackson, is copied *verbatim* from Allen's Reports.

"Jackson *vs.* Phillips and others, 14 Allen, 539.

"A bequest to trustees, to be expended at their discretion, 'in such sums, at such times and such places as they deem best, for the preparation and circulation of books, newspapers, the delivery of speeches, lectures and such other means as in their judgment will create a public sentiment that will put an end to negro slavery in this country,' was a legal charity before slavery was abolished in the United States.

"A bequest to trustees, to be expended at their discretion 'for the benefit of fugitive slaves who may escape from the slaveholding states of this infamous Union, from time to time,' might, before slavery was abolished in the United States, be lawfully applied, consistently with the expressed intention of the testator, to the relief of fugitive slaves in distress, or the extinguishment by purchase of the claims of those alleging themselves to be their masters, and was a legal charity.

"A bequest to trustees 'to secure the passage of laws granting women. whether married or unmarried, the right to vote, to hold office, to hold, manage and devise property, and all other civil rights enjoyed by men,' is not a charity."

"Bill in equity by the executor of the will of Francis Jackson, of Boston, for instructions as to the validity and effect of the following bequests and devises:

"Art. 6th. 'I give and bequeath to Wendell Phillips of said Boston, Lucy Stone, formerly of Brookfield, Mass., now the wife of Henry Blackwell of New York, and Susan B. Anthony of Rochester, N. Y., their successors and assigns, five thousand dollars, not for their own use, but in trust, nevertheless, to be expended by them without any responsibility to any one, at their discretion, in such sums, at such times and in such places as they may deem fit, to secure the passage of laws granting women, whether married or unmarried, the right to vote, to hold office, to hold, manage and devise property, and all other civil rights enjoyed by men, and for the preparation and circulation of books, the delivery of lectures, and such other means as they may judge best; and I hereby constitute them a board of trustees for that intent and purpose, with power to add two other persons to said board if they deem it expedient. And I hereby appoint Wendell Phillips president and treasurer, and Susan B. Anthony secretary of said board. I direct the treasurer of said board not to loan any part of said bequest, but to invest, and if need be, sell and re-invest the same in bank or railroad shares, at his discretion. I further authorize and request said board of trustees, the survivor and survivors of them, to fill any and all vacancies that may occur from time to time by death or resignation of any member or any officer of said board. One other bequest, hereinafter made, will, sooner or later, revert to this board of trustees. My desire is that they may become a permanent organization, until the rights of women shall be established equal with those of men; and I hope and trust that said board will receive the services and sympathy, the donations and bequests, of the friends of human rights. And being desirous that said board should have the immediate benefit of said bequest, without waiting for my exit, I have already paid it in advance and in full to said Phillips, the treasurer of said board, whose receipt therefor is on my files.'"

Gray, J. IV. "It is quite clear that the bequest in trust to be expended 'to secure the passage of laws granting women, whether married or unmarried, the right to vote, to hold office, to hold, manage and devise property, and all other civil rights enjoyed by men,' cannot be sustained as a charity. No precedent has been cited in its support. This bequest differs from the others, in aiming directly and exclusively to change the laws; and its object cannot be accomplished without changing the Constitution also. Whether such an alteration of the existing laws and frame of government would be wise and desirable, is a question upon which we cannot, sitting in a judicial capacity, properly express any opinion. Our duty is limited to expounding the laws as they stand. And those laws do not recognize the purpose of overthrowing or changing them, in whole or in part, as a charitable use. This bequest, therefore, not being for a charitable purpose, nor for the benefit of any particular persons, and being unrestricted in point of time, is inoperative and void. For the same reason, the gift to the same object, of one-third of the residue of the testator's estate after the death of his daughter, Mrs. Eddy, and her daughter, Mrs. Bacon, is also invalid, and will go to his heirs at law as a resulting trust."

Decision third and last was on the right of women to hold judicial offices. To quote again from Allen's Reports:

"On June 8, 1871, the following order was passed by the Governor and Council, and on June 10 transmitted to the Justices of the Supreme Judicial Court, who, on June 29, returned the reply which is annexed. Ordered, that the opinion of the Supreme Judicial Court be requested as to the following questions: First. Under the Constitution of this Commonwealth, can a woman, if duly appointed and qualified as a justice of the peace, legally perform all acts appertaining to that office? Second. Under the laws of this Commonwealth, would oaths and acknowledgments of deeds, taken before a married or unmarried woman duly appointed and qualified as a justice of the peace, be legal and valid?

OPINION.

"By the Constitution of the Commonwealth, the office of justice of the peace is a judicial office, and must be exercised by the officer in person, and a woman, whether married or unmarried, cannot be appointed to such an office.

"The law of Massachusetts at the time of the adoption of the Constitution, the whole frame and purport of the instrument itself, and the universal understanding and unbroken practical construction for the greater part of a century

afterwards, all support this conclusion, and are inconsistent with any other. It follows that, if a woman should
be formally appointed and commissioned as a justice of the
peace, she would have no constitutional or legal authority
to exercise any of the functions appertaining to that office.
Each of the questions proposed must, therefore, be respectfully answered in the negative.

(Signed),   REUBEN A. CHAPMAN,
              HORACE GRAY, Jr.,
              JOHN WELLS,
              JAMES D. COLT,
              SETH AMES,
              MARCUS MORTON.

"Boston, June 29, 1871."

M.

LUCY DOWNING AND HARVARD COLLEGE.

In a volume of old letters of the Winthrop family, published by the Massachusetts Historical Society, can be
found some very interesting facts concerning the part taken
by a woman in the inception of the first school or college
in the State. This lady was Lucy Downing, a sister of
Gov. Winthrop, the first governor of Massachusetts. She
was the wife of Emmanuel Downing, a lawyer of the Inner
Temple, a friend of Gov. Winthrop, and afterwards a man
of mark in the infant colony.

Mr. Downing and his wife remained in England some
years after John Winthrop came to New England, and
these early letters are written from that place. In one of
these letters to her brother, Lucy Downing expresses the
desire of herself and husband to come to New England
with their children, but laments that if they do come her
son George cannot complete his studies. She adds: "You

have yet no societies nor means of that kind for the education of youths in learning." She goes on to express her
solicitation in the matter and says: "It would make me
goe far nimbler to New England, if God should call me to
it, than otherwise I should, and I believe a colledge would
put noe small life into the plantation." This letter was
written early in 1636, and in October of the same year, the
General Court of the Massachusetts colony agreed to give
400 pounds towards establishing a school or college in
Newtowne, (two years afterwards called Cambridge.) Soon
afterwards Rev. John Harvard died and left one half of
his estate to this "infant seminary," and in 1638 it was
ordered by the General Court that the "Colledge to be
built at Cambridge shall be called Harvard Colledge."

Whether Lucy Downing's earnest plea to her brother,
the then powerful Governor of New England, for a school
in which to educate her son, prompted him, or hurried his
attention thus early to act in this direction, we cannot now
tell. It is as the history says "certainly a remarkable
coincidence" Early in 1638 Lucy Downing and her husband arrived in New England, and the name of George
Downing stands second on the list of the first class of
Harvard graduates in 1642. The Downings had other
sons who do not seem to have been educated at Harvard,
and daughters who were put out to service. One of these
daughters was married, or given in marriage, against her
own wishes, for she preferred at least two lovers to the man
chosen by her parents to be her husband. The son, for
whom so much was done by his mother, was afterwards
known as Sir George Downing, and he became rich and
powerful in England. Downing street in London is named
for him. In after life he forgot his duty to his mother, who
so naturally looked to him for support; and her last letter
written from England after her husband died, when she
was old and feeble, tells a sad story of her son's avarice and
meanness, and leaves the painful impression that she suffered in her old age for the necessaries of life.

It is a pathetic story, and one that has been told by many women since Lucy Downing's day. "I am now att ten pounde a yeare for mv chamber, and three pounde for my servants' wages, and have to extend the other ten pounde a yeare to accommodat for our meat and drink, and for my clothing and all other nessessaries I am much to seek, and more your brother Georg will not hear of for me, and he says that it is only covetousness that makes me ask more. He last summer bought another town near Hatly, calld Clappum, cost him thirteen or fourteen thousand pounds, and I really beleeve one of us two are indeed covetous." Then the poor old lady goes on to tell the high price of coal and wheat, and sends word to her nephew, John Winthrop, Jr., to see if he cannot help her in her want while she lives, and after her death help her daughter Peters (one of those who·went out to service), who she says plaintively "never yet had any portion, and to her I am sure it will not be offensive to my son Georg, whilst the principal remains to him, it being his patrimonie."

This letter was shown to John Winthrop, Jr., and he wrote at once a long letter to Sir George, begging him to make some suitable provision for his mother "aunt Lucy in her tyme of age and infirmity," and to settle upon her about an hundred pounds as annuity. Sir George in a short note replied, that it was not in his power to do more for his mother than he was already doing, that his means were not so large as was supposed, nor had he nearly as much money as people thought. The sequel shows, however, that he died very wealthy, and that the accumulated wealth of his family during their generations was finally used to establish a college in Cambridge, England.

At the present time it is hard to estimate how much influence the earnest longing of this one woman for the better education of her son, had in the founding of this earliest college in Massachusetts. But for her thinking and speaking at the right time, the enterprise might have been delayed for half a century. It is to be deplored that Lucy

Downing established the unwise precedent of educating óne member of her family at the expense of the rest ; a precedent followed by too many women since her time. Harvard College itself has followed it as well, in that it has so long excluded from its privileges, that portion of the human family to which Lucy Downing belongs.

Although women have never been permitted to become students of this college, or of any of the schools connected with it, yet they have always taken a great interest in its pecuniary welfare, and the university is largely indebted to the generosity of women for its endowment and support. From the annual reports and other records of Harvard College, it appears that since its foundation, funds have been contributed by one hundred and sixty-seven women which amount in the aggregate to $325,000. Out of these funds a proportion of the university scholarships were founded, and at least one of its professors' chairs. In its Divinity School alone, five of the ten scholarships bear the names of women. Caroline A. Plummer of Salem gave $15,000 to found the Plummer Professorship of Christian Morals. Sarah Derby bequeathed $1,000 towards founding the Hersey Professorship of Anatomy and Physic. The Holden Chapel was built with money given for that purpose by Mrs. Holden (widow of Samuel Holden) and her daughters. Anna E. P. Sever in 1879 left a legacy to this College of $140,000.

The names of other women benefactors of Harvard University are Lady Moulson, Hannah Sewall, Mary Saltonstall, Dorothy Saltonstall, Joanna Alford, Mary P. Townsend, Ann Toppan, Eliza Farrar, Ann F. Schaeffer, Levina Hoar, Rebecca A. Perkins, Caroline Merriam, Sarah Jackson, Hannah C. Andrews, Nancy Kendall, Charlotte Harris, Mary Osgood, Lucy Osgood, Sarah Winslow, Julia Bullock, Marian Hovey, Anna Richmond, Caroline Richmond, Clara J. Moore, Susan Cabot, and others.

The treasurer of the " Harvard Annex " in his annual report declares the great need that exists for funds to provide a suitable building, books, etc, for the numerous women students who continue to apply there for admission; and he appeals to the generosity of the public, for contributions of money to be used for this purpose. The casual observer might suggest that those women who will hereafter become the benefactors of this university, should remember the needs of their own sex, and leave their donations or bequests, so that they can be used for the benefit of the "Harvard Annex" and its students.

N.

THE ISLE OF MAN.

THIS most ancient kingdom does not send members to the British Parliament. It has its own government, its own House of Lords (the Council) and House of Commons (the Keys). It enacts its own laws, and imposes its own taxes, the only control being the sanction of the Queen. The House of Keys is a much older institution than the English House of Commons. It was established by a Scandinavian prince named Orry, about the year 938.

On Nov. 5, 1880, a "Franchise Bill" to secure further privileges to voters was introduced into the House of Keys. In committee of the House Mr. Richard Sherwood moved an amendment to strike out the word "male." This was done by the honorable member for the purpose of extending the franchise to women who possessed the required property qualifications. This amendment was carried by a two-thirds vote, and the Bill was signed by the Queen, Jan. 5, 1881. It could not, however, become a law, until, in accordance with immemorial custom, it was officially announced in the open air from the top of Tynwald Hill. This event took place Jan. 31, 1881. In March following, out of the 700 women electors on the island, 460 voted under the new law. At several of the polling stations, the women were the first to vote; and they were all received most cordially. Mr. Farrant who made a speech after the close of the election said: "The more we have of the women voters the better." Mr. Sherwood was one of the candidates for the house of Keys and of course received every woman's vote. In his address to his constituents he said, substantially: "On my nomination in this court, about eleven years ago, I was asked what I thought about female suffrage. I am glad to say that since then, we have achieved that, and that the first voter at the Ayer election was a woman. The subject of woman suffrage has brought the Isle of Man more prominently before many countries, than anything that has ever taken place. It turns out that we are the first Legislature in Europe which has extended the privilege to women. There is no doubt they will follow up the movement in England and perhaps before twelve months." The women voters in the Isle of Man received hearty congratulations from leading suffragists of England because of the proud position occupied by them in being the first women within Her Majesty's dominions whose rights as parliamentary electors have been recognized and legally secured.

In May, 1881, the Parliament of the United Kingdom passed the Municipal Franchise bill for the women of Scotland, and the act received the royal assent on June 3. After January, 1882, the women of that portion of the United Kingdom, will be legally entitled to vote in the elections of every Municipal Council. This is a great step towards establishing Parliamentary Franchise in Scotland.

Last of all to come into line is despotic Austria. In July, 1881, a new electoral law was proclaimed in Croatia, a province of Austria, by which women were called upon to vote in the forthcoming general election of Municipal Councils. Good news also, continues to come from Italy. Two girl students of the Roman University — Carolina Magistrelli and Evangelina Bottero — who had passed with great distinction examinations in Greek, Latin and Italian literature, have recently taken doctors' degrees in the Natural Sciences. The Rome *Opinione* says, that so far as is known, no woman has, until now, taken a degree in the Roman University, since its foundation by Innocent IV. in the thirteenth century.

In 1650, when Anne Bradstreet lived and wrote her verses, a woman author was almost unknown in English Literature. This lady was the wife of the Governor of Massachusetts, and because of her literary tendencies, was looked upon by the people of her time as a marvel of womankind. Her contemporaries called her the "tenth muse lately sprung up in America," and one of them, Rev. Nathaniel Ward, was inspired to write an address to her, in which he declares his wonder at her success as a poet, and playfully foretells the consequences, if women are permitted to intrude farther into the domain of man. The closing lines express so well the conflicting emotions which torment the minds of the opponents of the Woman Suffrage movement, that I venture to quote them, as an appropriate ending to this book:

" ' Good sooth,' quoth the old Don, ' tell ye me so
  I muse whither at length these Girls will go.
  It half revives my chil, frost-bitten blood
  To see a woman once do aught that's good
  And Chode by Chaucer's Boots and Homer's Furrs
  Let men look to't, least Women wear the Spurrs.' "

INDEX.

A

Adams, Abigail and John, 8, 9.

Advancement of Women, Association for, sketch of, 158, 159.

Agitator, The (early woman's rights paper), 63.

Alcott, A. Bronson, 16, 37, 67, 232.

Alcott, Abby M., 92, 93, 232.

Alexander, Janet, 134.

American Equal Rights Association, formed, 45; first convention (1866), 46; first anniversary, 52; changed to National Woman Suffrage Association (1869), 47.

American Woman Suffrage Association, formed, 47, 51; conventions of, 55.

Andrew, John A., suggestion concerning the surplus women in Massachusetts, 98.

Anneke, Madame (of Germany), 29.

Anthony, Susan B., first appearance (1852), 27, 28; early connection with the movement, 30, 37; later, 45, 46, 55, 56.

Anti-Slavery Convention (World's), 14; account of, 190.

Anti-Slavery Society (American), 11; women allowed to speak and vote at conventions of, 12; women allowed to be officers of, 13; division of, 13. (see Garrisonian Wing; also Appendix B.)

Anti-Slavery Society (Boston Female), 11.

Anti-Slavery Society (New England), 12.

Art, woman in, 151.

F.

Farley, Harriet, 17, 153. (*see* Appendix C).

Ferrin, Mary Upton, 237.

Foley, Margaret, 151, 152 (*see* Appendix C).

Folsom, Abby, 11.

Foster, Abby Kelley (*see* Kelley), early connection with the movement, 20, 22, 30, 36, 232; speech at Worcester (1851), 26; later, 48, 55, 61. (*see* Appendixes B and H).

Foster, Stephen S., early connection with the movement, 14, 22, 30; later, 45, 48, 55, 67.

France, woman's rights in, 182.

Fuller, Margaret, influence of the early writings of, 15, 153; death of, 21.

G.

Gage, Frances D., 26, 30, 37, 45, 61.

Gage, Matilda E. Joslyn, 28.

Garrison, William Lloyd, early connection with the movement, 14, 22, 24, 28, 30, 36, 232; later, 48, 63, 96, 220. (*see* Appendix B).

Garrisonian Wing of American Anti-Slavery Society, 13, 15. (*see* Appendix B).

Giddings, Joshua R., 31.

Gove, Mary S., 10.

Greeley, Horace, 28, 37.

Greene, William B., 95.

Grimké, Angelina, first appearance of 10, 115; early connection with the movement, 12, 15, 26, 28; later, 86.

Grimké, Sarah, early connection with the movement, 10, 11, 12, 15; later, 86.

H.

Hampden County Society formed, 51, 52.

Hampshire County Society formed, 51.

17

M.

N.

S.

CPSIA information can be obtained at www.ICGtesting.com
Printed in the USA
BVOW06s1452070416

443360BV00027B/441/P